If Your Adolescent Has an Eating Disorder

THE ANNENBERG
PUBLIC POLICY CENTER
OF THE UNIVERSITY OF PENNSYLVANIA

Daniel Romer, PhD, Director of Research

The Annenberg Foundation Trust at
SUNNYLANDS

The Adolescent Mental Health Initiative of the Annenberg
Public Policy Center and the Sunnylands Trust

Patrick E. Jamieson, Ph.D., series editor

Other books in the series

If Your Adolescent Has Depression or Bipolar Disorder
Dwight L. Evans, M.D., and Linda Wasmer Andrews

If Your Adolescent Has Schizophrenia
Raquel E. Gur, M.D., Ph.D., and Ann Braden Johnson, Ph.D.

If Your Adolescent Has an Anxiety Disorder
Edna B. Foa, Ph.D., and Linda Wasmer Andrews

If Your Adolescent Has ADHD
Tomas J. Power, Ph.D., and Linda Wasmer Andrews

If Your Adolescent Has an Eating Disorder

An Essential Resource for Parents

SECOND EDITION

B. Timothy Walsh
Deborah R. Glasofer

THE ANNENBERG
PUBLIC POLICY CENTER
OF THE UNIVERSITY OF PENNSYLVANIA

The Adolescent Mental Health Initiative of the Annenberg
Public Policy Center and the Sunnylands Trust

The Annenberg Foundation Trust at
SUNNYLANDS

OXFORD
UNIVERSITY PRESS

OXFORD
UNIVERSITY PRESS

Oxford University Press is a department of the University of Oxford. It furthers
the University's objective of excellence in research, scholarship, and education
by publishing worldwide. Oxford is a registered trade mark of Oxford University
Press in the UK and certain other countries.

Published in the United States of America by Oxford University Press
198 Madison Avenue, New York, NY 10016, United States of America.

© Oxford University Press 2020

Library of Congress Cataloging-in-Publication Data
Names: Walsh, B. Timothy, 1946- author. | Glasofer, Deborah R., 1979- author.
Title: If your adolescent has an eating disorder : an essential resource
for parents / B. Timothy Walsh, Deborah R. Glasofer, The Adolescent
Mental Health Initiative of the Annenberg Public Policy Center and the
Sunnylands Trust.
Description: Second edition. | New York : Oxford University Press, [2020] |
Series: Adolescent mental health initiative | Includes bibliographical
references and index.
Identifiers: LCCN 2019053402 (print) | LCCN 2019053403 (ebook) |
ISBN 9780190076825 (paperback) | ISBN 9780190076849 (epub)
Subjects: LCSH: Eating disorders in adolescence—Popular works.
Classification: LCC RJ506.E18 W36 2020 (print) | LCC RJ506.E18 (ebook) |
DDC 616.85/2600835—dc23
LC record available at https://lccn.loc.gov/2019053402
LC ebook record available at https://lccn.loc.gov/2019053403

9 8 7 6 5 4 3 2 1
Printed by LSC Communications, United States of America

Contents

Six

Acknowledgments

We are grateful to the following colleagues for their contributions and feedback: Evelyn Attia, MD; Eve Freidl, MD; Nikki Pagano, LCSW; Sarah Parker, PhD; and Lisa Ranzenhofer, PhD.

About the Authors

B. Timothy Walsh, MD, is Ruane Professor of Pediatric Psychopharmacology in the Vagelos College of Physicians & Surgeons at the Columbia University Irving Medical Center and founder of the Columbia Center for Eating Disorders at the New York State Psychiatric Institute. He chaired the Adolescent Mental Health Initiative's formal Commission on Eating Disorders, a blue-ribbon panel of leading authorities convened in 2017 to assess the current research on these disorders; the findings of Dr. Walsh's commission make up the scientific foundation of this book.

Deborah R. Glasofer, PhD, is Associate Professor of Clinical Medical Psychology (in Psychiatry) at the Columbia University Irving Medical Center and clinical psychologist at the Columbia Center for Eating Disorders at the New York State Psychiatric Institute. She is involved in research on eating and weight disorders in adults and adolescents and provides instruction and supervision for clinical trainees in cognitive behavioral therapy for mood, anxiety, and eating disorders. She has written for *Scientific American Mind, Psychology Today, The Huffington Post, Verywell,* and *The Feed* and can be followed on Twitter at @drglasofer.

Chapter One

Introduction

Not Just a Diet

When Susan told her husband Ted that their daughter Vanessa had been diagnosed with anorexia nervosa, he was actually relieved. "In hindsight, it sounds terrible," she says. "But because our daughter was eating very little and had lost so much weight, we feared the worst. So, when he heard 'eating disorder,' his reaction was to say, 'Fine. Now all we have to do is make her eat.' Unfortunately, we've since learned just how horrible eating disorders can be and how long it takes to recover from one."

Like Susan and Ted, many parents know very little about eating disorders, and, when first learning their child has one, they may not know how to react. Some may think that their child can be easily "fixed" simply by forcing her or him to eat. Others may think their child has a deep-seated emotional problem that will take years of intensive therapy to uncover. Still others may wonder if their child's problem is just another "fad" diet spreading through the ranks of her or his friends. And still others may feel like Shirley did when she found out her daughter Jody had bulimia nervosa: "I felt immense shame—I could not believe that a daughter of *mine* would do such a thing to herself. You see, I thought bulimia was a choice. If one could choose to begin the behavior, then one could choose to end it as well. Due to the shame and the stigma—our culture reinforces this notion that spoiled young women choose to have an eating disorder—it was difficult for me to admit to all but my closest friends what was happening within our family."

> "I could not believe that a daughter of mine would do such a thing to herself."

This variety of reactions reflects the fact that the term "eating disorder," even in the community of professionals who specialize in treating such disturbances, describes a broad spectrum of problems. Three eating disorders—anorexia nervosa, bulimia nervosa, and binge-eating disorder—are clearly defined and have been extensively studied. Anorexia nervosa and bulimia nervosa in particular are potentially life-threatening illnesses that predominantly affect young females but can also affect others regardless of age, gender, race, or economic background. Binge-eating disorder, though not life-threatening, creates significant distress for the affected individual and, in some cases, can have an impact on lifelong weight trajectory. Avoidant/restrictive food intake disorder (ARFID) is a relatively newly recognized condition to join the list of eating disorders, and its features are therefore even less familiar to the general public.

Of note, eating disorder specialists recognize that many young people have significant eating problems that interfere with normal physical and emotional development but are not quite full-blown eating disorders. In addition, many more young people develop unusual eating habits and food preferences that are peculiar but transient and harmless, as Anne's experience with her daughter, Charlotte, demonstrates.

As a child, Charlotte had eaten everything put in front of her, but when she turned 13, she suddenly refused to eat anything except a certain few foods that didn't exactly create a balanced diet. Anne tried to encourage her to eat other things, but nothing else would do. If her favorite foods weren't on the menu (either at home or elsewhere), Charlotte preferred to go hungry.

A former ice skater who'd won numerous awards at amateur competitions, Anne had aspired to join a professional ice show but gave up her dream when she saw how other skaters starved themselves or used diuretics or laxatives to meet the required weight limit. To her, skating was something she loved doing, but not to the point where it might do physical harm. Having witnessed her former colleagues' unhealthy behaviors, she became concerned about Charlotte's food restrictions and took her daughter to a physician who specialized in eating disorders. Upon hearing Anne's concerns, the doctor performed a physical examination followed by a blood test. Then, and most importantly (according to Anne), he had a long talk with Charlotte and advised Anne to do the same. In the end, neither doctor nor mother could find any physical or psychological evidence that Charlotte was experiencing anything other than a change in her tastes. She proved to be a self-assured, robust, healthy teenager who just happened to like only certain foods. Charlotte eventually went off to college, got married, and had kids of her own who now frequently bedevil her with what they will or won't eat.

While the onset of eating disorders usually occurs around the start of or soon after puberty, not all teenagers who alter their eating habits should be immediately suspect. As parents know from having been teenagers themselves, adolescence is a turbulent time that brings with it added social and academic pressures as well as physiological changes. Consequently, a formerly voracious eater might suddenly become a picky one, an increase in school or extracurricular activities can cause kids to miss family meals, and all those "raging hormones" can make teenagers focus more on their appearance.

Adolescence is a turbulent time that brings with it added social and academic pressures as well as physiological changes.

Adriana, whose daughter Cristina developed anorexia nervosa, recalls, "When your daughter first goes on a diet, you think, 'Well, okay, everybody diets.' I certainly did when I was young, mostly because all of my friends were doing it. That's why I didn't say anything to Cristina when she went on a diet. She's really smart and I knew that, given time, she'd figure it all out and give up the dieting thing, too. Unfortunately, that wasn't the case, and I now deeply regret not talking to her sooner."

As the previous illustrations demonstrate, the wide range of human food preferences and consumption can make the recognition of a serious eating disorder difficult. This is particularly true during adolescence, when kids require more energy to support their bodies' normal growth and development. According to a 2015 report on Dietary Guidelines for Americans from the US Department of Health and Human Services, the number of calories girls need to eat increases between the ages of 9 and 19 by almost 40% and for boys by 55%. Perhaps in part because of this dramatic biological imperative, combined with society's ever-changing notion of how one "should" look, it is common for teenagers to start dieting. These and other elements can create a fertile environment for the development of disordered eating, as the following statistics from the medical literature illustrate:

- A study published in 2019 found that although most adolescents felt that their weight was "about right," almost half of both boys and girls were trying to change it.
- A study published in 2011 reported that about half of girls and one-fourth of boys in early adolescence (on average, approximately 13 years old) said they had dieted in the past year.
- A survey conducted in the late 1990s found that more than half of adolescent girls and about one-quarter of adolescent boys reported engaging in unhealthy weight control behaviors.
- As of 2002, 56% percent of ninth-grade females and 28% of ninth-grade males reported binge eating or engaging in one or more of the following to lose or control weight: fasting or skipping meals, taking diet pills or laxatives, inducing vomiting, or smoking cigarettes. In a nationally representative sample of adolescents ages 16–19 queried between 2013 and 2016, 16.5% of those trying to lose weight did so by skipping meals.

Since the publication of the first edition of this book, various longitudinal studies (i.e., those that consider changes over extended time periods) have been published that underscore the importance of raising awareness about unhealthy eating and weight control behaviors and promoting early intervention:

- Of approximately 7,000 adolescents followed between 1998 and 2001, 8% of the girls initiated purging behavior, and 12% of the girls and 5% of the boys began to binge eat.

- According to a study published in 2011, an increase in extreme weight control behaviors was found in youth transitioning from adolescence to young adulthood over the course of a decade-long investigation. Specifically, diet pill use more than tripled, and one-fifth of female young adults reported the use of extreme weight control behaviors.

Taken together, these numbers highlight the very high rates of concern about weight control among youngsters and the strong wish, especially among girls, to lose weight. Fortunately, the most serious eating disorders are much less common. While there is substantial uncertainty about their prevalence, the general consensus among experts is that full-blown eating disorders occur in approximately 1% (anorexia nervosa) to 5% (binge-eating disorder) of women at some point during their lives, with the rates among men approximately one-tenth of those observed in women. And what about among teenagers? In a nationally representative sample of more than 10,000 adolescents ages 13–18 published in 2011, the lifetime prevalence rate of anorexia nervosa, bulimia nervosa, and binge-eating disorder was approximately 0.3%, 1%, and 1.6%, respectively. Because ARFID was formally introduced as an eating disorder diagnosis in 2013, there are few population studies describing its prevalence rates. While the rate of anorexia nervosa remains remarkably stable (for teens and adults alike), there are some data to suggest that the rate of bulimia nervosa in teens is dropping. In adolescents, up to 10% of all cases of eating disorders occur in males. Compared with the other eating disorders, binge-eating disorder is more common in adolescent boys.

More will be said later about how eating disorders are formally defined by experts and about how many young people develop them, but for now the key point we want to emphasize about the statistics on adolescents is this: all of these teenagers have a parent or parents who have had to face the impact of these disorders on their children's and on their own daily lives. They've all had questions about these illnesses: What are they? What causes them? What can make them go away? The scientific community of researchers on eating disorders has answers to these questions, and, while we have more answers to these questions than we did when the first edition of this book was published, most of the answers remain incomplete, relying on ongoing discovery about the causes, treatments, and prevention of these illnesses. Indeed, if you are the parent of a child with or at risk for an eating disorder, you likely have many more questions about your child than are possible to answer conclusively at this time. Our aim in this book is to give you the best scientific information on eating disorders that can currently be provided and to give you a sense of what you will likely encounter as you go about getting help for your child. Clearly, we cannot answer all your questions, nor can a book stand in the place of actual professional evaluation and treatment. But we can help you understand what your adolescent is going through and what you as a parent can do to help him or her recover.

The scientific material presented here draws in large part from the findings of a Commission on Eating Disorders, chaired by the lead author of this book, that was part of the Adolescent Mental Health Initiative spearheaded in 2003 by the Annenberg Foundation Trust at Sunnylands to address the increasing prevalence of severe mental illness (e.g., depression, anxiety disorders, eating disorders, and other conditions) among our nation's young people. This material was thoroughly updated in 2017. In addition, the book draws from other sources as well, most compellingly from parents who have faced these disorders in their own children. For a few of these parents, the struggle to save their children from the ravages of anorexia nervosa or bulimia nervosa was sadly lost. For others, the struggle continues to this day. And for still others, the battle with anorexia nervosa, bulimia nervosa, binge-eating disorder, or ARFID has been hard but ultimately triumphant. Regardless of outcome, they have all gone through something similar to what you're going through now. The case material included in this book is based on interviews with parents conducted for the first edition and now augmented by additional information from cases treated by the authors and by several colleagues. The names of all the people and their personal, potentially identifying information has been changed in order to protect their privacy, but the snapshots we describe are very real. Their experiences provide a wealth of practical wisdom and personal insights that we believe you'll find meaningful. We are exceedingly grateful to them for their courage and generosity in opening up their lives to us for this purpose.

> The book draws from other sources as well, most compellingly from parents who have faced these disorders in their own children.

Chapter Two

Understanding Eating Disorders

What They Are and What to Expect

Anorexia Nervosa

When Chelsey started skipping meals and isolating herself from family and friends, her parents began to worry. "As a young girl, she was always so outgoing," her mother, Donna, says. "She had lots of friends and was involved in all kinds of social activities. She was also an excellent student and a perfectionist. Everything had to be done just so and, if something wasn't done exactly the way she thought it should be, she'd become distressed and do it over and over again until she got it right. This perfectionistic attitude spilled over into her drive to be thin. When my husband and I finally told her she needed to stop dieting, she became angry and annoyed with us for interfering in her life. That really took us by surprise because she'd never spoken to us that way before. We later found out that she didn't just want to be thin, she wanted to be thinner than everyone else."

> "This perfectionistic attitude spilled over into her drive to be thin."

Valerie noticed similar changes in her daughter, Audra. "She became very withdrawn and secretive. She started acting as though there was some inner demon driving her to keep moving and stay busy. She suddenly became very preoccupied and had a short attention span. As she lost weight and her physical condition deteriorated, she also became extremely short-tempered and her thinking was irrational at times. When her weight reached the critical stage, she even became violent."

Diane's first clue that something was wrong with Michael came when her son returned home after his first year away at college. "He was extremely thin, always cold, and looked unhealthy," Diane recalls. "Plus, his relationship to food had completely changed. As a teenager, he'd always loved food. We would celebrate after his track meets by going to his favorite pizza place, and he was always eager to help his dad make pancakes or French toast for weekend family brunches. All that changed after he came back from school, and it was clear he was seeing food in a different way. He refused to go back to the pizza place or, if we could get him there, insisted on ordering salad instead of his old favorites. He suddenly agonized over what he could or couldn't eat, and grocery shopping or cooking at home turned into an exhausting ordeal because he had to calculate every calorie and fat gram or else up his running mileage that week. Many of the items he was willing to eat I would not even consider 'real' food, for example, high protein shakes or bars. He started spending a lot of time doing online research—reading blogs, watching YouTube videos, and checking Instagram for workouts that would make him lean and new smoothie recipes. His healthy relationship with food and exercise had changed to an unhealthy one, and trying to get him to eat anything or to skip a workout became a nightmare."

Chelsey, Audra, and Michael were all exhibiting signs and symptoms of *anorexia nervosa*, a complex mental disorder that can cause a person to literally "waste away" due to an intense fear of being fat. Even when at a dangerously low weight, a teen can refer to herself or himself as a "fat cow" because the disease distorts how people think about themselves.

Anorexia nervosa normally begins around the onset of puberty or a little after, and full-blown cases occur in about 1 in every 200 adolescents. Though undeniably more common in girls, teenage boys are also affected by this eating disorder and make up about 10% of cases. Anorexia nervosa is one of the deadliest psychiatric disorders, with a mortality rate estimated at 0.56% per year, or approximately 5.6% per decade. That rate is approximately 12 times higher than the annual death rate due to all causes of death among people between the ages 15 and 24 in the general population. Further discussion about the prevalence or frequency of anorexia nervosa appears later in this chapter, in the section, "How Common Are Eating Disorders in Adolescents?" (pp. 47–49).

By itself, the term *anorexia* actually means "loss of appetite." Virtually everyone has experienced anorexia: for example, the "stomach flu" and several medications, like some types of chemotherapy drugs, can produce an aversion to food and cause weight loss. Those with the mental disorder anorexia nervosa, however, do not have the same kind of aversion to food. In fact, they are almost always hungry and think about food constantly even as the disorder impels them to deny their bodies the fuel it needs to function properly. This denial of the normal desire for food can even include going to great lengths to "protect" the disease, such as avoiding social occasions involving meals, trying to hide severe weight loss by wearing baggy clothes, or lying to family and friends about what they are or aren't eating.

"It's hard to believe that your own kid would lie right to your face," Diane says, "especially if they've never done it before. So, when they say they had a big lunch or ate dinner with a friend, you believe them. There's nothing to tell you that you shouldn't. I mean, who wants to think their son is not only a liar but is purposely trying to starve himself to death?"

> "It's hard to believe that your own kid would lie right to your face."

While it is understandable that Diane experienced her son as lying to her in this context, it was anorexia nervosa, not him, who tried to mislead her. And while many children in the throes of anorexia nervosa do wind up starving themselves to a critical point physically, few set out with such a mission in mind. The disease can often take hold because they start out feeling betrayed by their changing bodies. With the onset of puberty, a girl suddenly has to deal with a figure that is becoming curvy—with growing breasts, hips, buttocks, and thighs—which may make her feel self-conscious. Likewise, an adolescent boy who grows wider instead of taller and more muscular might be the object of ridicule from his peers because his "baby fat" makes him look "chubby" instead of strong and lean. In our culture, a remarkably high percentage of both boys and girls are unhappy with their appearance. According to one study, approximately half of third- to fifth-grade children were dissatisfied by their weight, and most of the girls wanted to be thinner. The dissatisfaction with physical appearance suggested by such statistics, along with the mental and physical changes that accompany the onset of puberty, can trigger all kinds of disordered-eating behaviors in sensitive children who define much of their self-worth by how they look.

Additionally, when some kids do go on a diet and lose weight, they can become so intoxicated with what they have accomplished and with praise from friends or relatives (e.g., "Wow, you look great!" or "Man, that diet really worked, didn't it?") that they might think, "Well, if you think I look good now, just wait and see how good I look after I lose another 10 pounds."

Contrary to commonly held stereotypes about anorexia nervosa, there are a variety of ways—beyond highly restrictive eating—that people with this disorder try to control their weight. The more well-known subtype, the one classically depicted, is *restricting subtype*. However, approximately half of all individuals with anorexia nervosa have *binge-eating/purging subtype*, in which they experience regular episodes of out-of-control eating and/or purging (by self-induced vomiting, laxative use, etc.) while at a low body weight. As will be discussed shortly, individuals who regularly binge eat and purge but who are not significantly underweight meet criteria for a different eating disorder—*bulimia nervosa*—but those with anorexia nervosa can and do experience some of the same unusual eating and compensatory behaviors.

In cases of adolescent anorexia nervosa, it is also possible that weight loss in absolute pounds is not as dramatic as what it represents on a teen's growth curve. From infancy to early adulthood, internal and external construction is expected to occur, leading to growth in stature (i.e., height) and weight. This means that failure to make expected gains or even modest weight loss may signify a clinically meaningful deviation and possible malnourishment.

Audra, for example, always tracked at the 50th percentile for height and weight, calculated as *body mass index* (BMI) in the growth curve illustrated in Figure 2.1. BMI is a standardized measure of body size. It is calculated by dividing someone's

CDC Growth Charts: United States

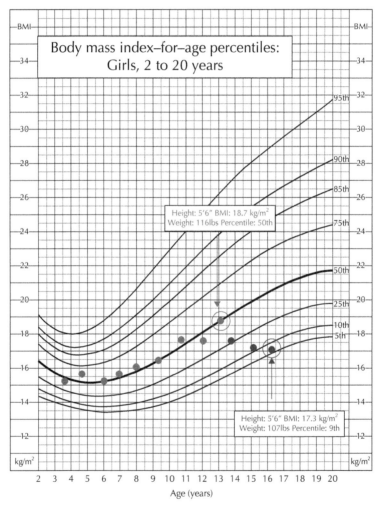

Figure 2.1 Sample growth curve of adolescent with anorexia nervosa.

weight (in kilograms) divided by their height (in meters) squared. Fortunately, it's easy to find calculators to do this on the internet, such as https://www.cdc.gov/healthyweight/ assessing/bmi/adult_bmi/english_bmi_calculator/bmi_cal- culator.html. For adults who have stopped growing, BMI is very easy to interpret and generally falls into one of four cat- egories: underweight (under 18.5), normal weight (18.5–25), overweight (25–30), and obese (over 30). For children and adolescents, interpretation is more difficult, so pediatricians often use a growth chart that shows how BMI changes with age. There is also a BMI calculator for youth, which takes into account exact age, available online at https://www.cdc.gov/ healthyweight/bmi/calculator.html. Based on a child's age, sex, height, and weight, this calculator figures out how the child's weight compares to that of other children of the same age and sex. A child whose BMI is at the 5th percentile or less is almost certainly underweight and should be evaluated by their pediatrician.

When Audra began to diet around age 13, she "fell off" of her body's natural growth trajectory (i.e., approximately the 50th BMI percentile). When her mother, Valerie, noticed the first psychological signs of an eating disorder, as described earlier, it was about a year later, and Audra's weight loss was relatively minimal. She had lost 7 pounds to a weight of 109 pounds, illustrated by first dot in Figure 2.1. Valerie was still quite concerned, as was Audra's pediatrician, who began to fol- low her growth more closely. Audra was resistant to her moth- er's efforts to get her into treatment initially, but by the time she was 16 and displaying changes in her temperament and inclinations to be violent when upset, Valerie and the pediatri- cian were insistent. When Audra was first seen by an eating disorders specialist, she was 107 pounds—less than 10 pounds lower from her weight at age 13. However, Audra had neither grown taller over those 3 years nor had she made expected weight *gains*. Her BMI percentile had therefore dropped from the 50th to the 7th. A major goal of Audra's treatment was to get her back on her expected growth curve. Looking at the growth curve chart, it's easy to see that the weight to aim for will change as someone gets taller as they get better. Furthermore, since there is no single "perfect" weight for anyone, it's best to think of a target weight range. We will come back to this topic in Chapter 3 when we discuss treatment.

Unfortunately, no matter the degree of weight loss, when a teen vulnerable to anorexia nervosa becomes burdened with the drive to be thin or to maintain thinness, it can spiral quickly into an obsession. One adolescent even described herself as a "soldier" in the fight not to succumb to the enemy (hunger), with every second, every minute, and every hour of her life being driven by the need to win the "war" waged between her body and her need to control it.

Public awareness about anorexia nervosa has increased dramatically in the past few decades, in part because of the media's focus on celebrities with eating disorders. Recent disclosures have come from female entertainers including Lady Gaga and Demi Lovato, both of whom shared histories of severe food restriction and self-induced vomiting beginning in their teen years. Several well-known men have also spoken and written candidly about eating disorders that started in early adolescence, including *New York Times* writer Frank Bruni and comedian Russell Brand. One of the earliest examples occurred in 1983, when Grammy Award–winning pop singer Karen Carpenter died of heart failure at the age of 32 as a result of the long-term effects of self-starvation, self-induced vomiting, and laxative abuse.

"At the time I was completely shocked," says a mother whose daughter died of an eating disorder some 15 years later. "How could someone as rich and famous as Karen Carpenter die at such a young age simply because she'd gone on a diet? Back then we really didn't understand the difference between just dieting and having an eating disorder. Her death made headlines all over the country, but they only said she'd died because her heart gave out, making us think that it was a biological or genetic problem. It wasn't until years later—when my own daughter was diagnosed—that I was finally able to learn more about how insidious eating disorders really are."

Although anorexia nervosa has been recognized as a medical condition for centuries, mental health professionals were just beginning to describe it in a coherent and consistent way at the time of Carpenter's death in 1983. Before the mid-1970s, psychiatric illnesses were characterized for the most part in very broad terms, like *neurosis*, that were based on concepts from psychoanalysis. Then, in the 1970s, a profound revolution occurred in how psychiatric disorders were described and labeled. The profession shifted from characterizing disorders on the basis of the psychoanalytic theory of unconscious conflicts to categorizing behavioral and emotional problems on the basis of characteristics that are much easier to observe and describe. So the term *neurosis* was eliminated as an officially recognized diagnosis and was replaced by a large number of much more specific categories, including anorexia nervosa. This dramatic shift in how mental health professionals describe and name the illnesses they treat culminated in 1980, with the publication by the American Psychiatric Association of the *Diagnostic and Statistical Manual of Mental Disorders*, Third Edition, also referred to as *DSM-III*. The current version of this book, the *Diagnostic and Statistical Manual of Mental*

Disorders (Fifth Edition, 2013), or *DSM-5*, lists all of the officially recognized psychiatric disorders, including anorexia nervosa, bulimia nervosa, binge-eating disorder, and ARFID and is extremely important in influencing practitioners, researchers, and even insurance companies.

In developing the *DSM*, mental health practitioners have followed the tradition of the broader medical profession. Over many centuries, doctors have moved toward more and more specific definitions of illnesses, from describing a patient as having "fever and cough" to having "pneumococcal pneumonia." This transition has been useful for a variety of reasons, not the least of which is that it allows doctors to develop and provide much more specific and effective treatments. But a major difference still exists between the diagnosis of medical and psychiatric illnesses. The diagnosis of a psychiatric illness is based almost exclusively on the patient's (and the family's) description of the problem, such as the occurrence of troublesome thoughts, behaviors, and feelings, and the clinician's observations of the patient. In other areas of medicine, descriptions of symptoms, like complaints of pain, provide the first indications of the nature of the illness, but the final diagnosis is almost always confirmed by some other means, such as blood tests or sophisticated imaging procedures like magnetic resonance imaging (MRIs) or computed tomography (CAT) scans. Such confirmatory diagnostic tests are not yet available for psychiatric illnesses, including anorexia nervosa, so doctors must arrive at a diagnosis by relying on the description of the patient's problem, their observations of the patient, and their own experience and judgment.

Some tests *can* reveal certain physical signs of eating disorders, such as low heart rate and blood pressure, dehydration, or electrolyte imbalances. But the key to making a diagnosis of anorexia nervosa involves keen observation, and, to that end, parents can play a major role by watching for certain outward signs and symptoms, such as

- A dramatic weight loss not associated with a medical illness
- Self-deprecating remarks about being too fat despite noticeable weight loss
- A preoccupation with food, calories, and fat content
- Restrictive eating habits that begin with the refusal to eat certain foods and progress to the elimination of whole categories of foods (e.g., fats, carbohydrates)
- Inducing vomiting after eating (this is a cardinal symptom of bulimia nervosa, but it also occurs in about 50% of individuals with anorexia nervosa)
- Development of eating rituals (e.g., rearranging food on a plate to make it look like more has been eaten than actually has, cutting food into tiny bites, chewing food for an excessively long period, or eating foods in a certain order)
- Behavior indicating that weight loss, dieting, and control of food intake have become a primary concern
- Denial of hunger despite substantial loss of weight or failure to gain as expected
- Wearing baggy clothes to hide extreme weight loss
- The avoidance of family meals and other social occasions that involve food
- The need to follow a rigid (usually excessive) exercise routine despite bad weather, injury, or illness
- Social isolation and withdrawal from family and friends
- Secretiveness, hostility, intolerance, and irritability
- Difficulty concentrating
- Weakness, faintness, or blackouts (in conjunction with other symptoms)

If you think your son or daughter is at risk for anorexia nervosa because he or she is exhibiting these signs, it is important to take them seriously and to act quickly to get your child help. These symptoms do not in themselves represent a formal diagnosis of the illness, but they are "red flags" that indicate your child needs to see a medical professional immediately. That professional will in turn assess your teen's symptoms in light of formal criteria or guidelines, likely to be those set forth in *DSM-5*. These criteria are shown in Table 2.1 and are further

Table 2.1 Diagnostic Criteria for Anorexia Nervosa

A. Restriction of energy intake relative to requirements, leading to a significantly low body weight in the context of age, sex, developmental trajectory, and physical health. *Significantly low weight* is defined as a weight that is less than minimally normal or, for children and adolescents, less than that minimally expected.

B. Intense fear of gaining weight or becoming fat, or persistent behavior that interferes with weight gain, even though at a significantly low weight.

C. Disturbance in the way in which one's body weight or shape is experienced, undue influence of body weight or shape on self-evaluation, or persistent lack of recognition of the seriousness of the current low body weight.

Specify type:

Restricting type: during the last 3 months, the individual has not engaged in recurrent episodes of binge eating or purging behavior (i.e., self-induced vomiting or the misuse of laxatives, diuretics, or enemas). This subtype describes presentations in which the weight loss is accomplished primarily through dieting, fasting, and/or excessive exercise.

Binge-eating/Purging type: during the last 3 months, the individual has engaged in recurrent episodes of binge eating or purging behavior (i.e., self-induced vomiting or the misuse of laxatives, diuretics, or enemas).

Source: Reprinted by permission from the *Diagnostic and Statistical Manual of Mental Disorders* (2013). American Psychiatric Association.

discussed in the section called "What Does a *DSM* Diagnosis Mean?" (pp. 36–47).

Bulimia Nervosa

"Food was always a big part of Linda's life," Kay says of her daughter, who was diagnosed with bulimia nervosa. "Even when she was in kindergarten, she would take a box of cereal or crackers, go sit in front of the TV, and eat out of the box. She was also larger and more developed than most kids her age. As time went on, she became self-conscious about her size."

A month before Linda turned 12, she got the stomach flu, was out of school for a week, and lost 10 pounds. "When Linda returned to school," Kay says, "she got so much attention for losing weight that she decided to lose more. Eventually, she stopped eating anything but oranges. We kept trying to get her to eat, but nothing worked, and after 4 months, she'd lost 50 pounds. Then she suddenly started eating again. We were thrilled, but we were also amazed because she wasn't gaining any weight." She also began spending more and more time in the bathroom, and, when Kay would go in to clean up, it appeared as if someone had vomited. Kay noticed changes in Linda's moods, too.

"After 4 months, she'd lost 50 pounds."

"Suddenly she wasn't our sweet, easygoing kid anymore. She started having trouble getting along with her sisters and grandmother, plus we also noticed lots of food disappearing. I would get home from the store and swear I had bought bagels, but the next morning when I went to look for them, they would be gone. I asked everybody in the house where they were, and they all claimed they hadn't seen them. I started questioning whether the bagels had even made it home from the grocery store or if I had accidentally left them in the basket or on the counter."

According to Kay, Linda was also not the neatest person in the world and arguments about her room always being a mess were frequent. An agreement was finally struck that, if Linda wanted to leave it that way, she'd have to keep her bedroom door closed and would be responsible for putting away her clothes after they were laundered. After Linda left for camp the following summer, Kay went into Linda's room to give it a thorough cleaning.

"I found all these clothes that she'd purged in. They were shoved into drawers, under the bed, and stuffed in her soccer bag. There were enough clothes to fill a large lawn-size garbage bag. How there wasn't an incredible stench in that room is still beyond me. And a lot of the purging was dark matter, which I later found out from professionals was bile because that was how hard she was purging."

Linda exhibited classic symptoms of bulimia nervosa, a disease that was first clearly recognized as a disorder by the psychiatric community in 1979. It is characterized by episodes of binge eating large quantities of food during a short period of time, followed by purging (most commonly via self-induced vomiting, but laxatives and diuretics—fluid pills—are also used), restricting food intake (via fasting or extreme dieting), or exercising excessively: all in an effort to avoid gaining weight from the binge eating. When vomiting is used, such binges can be repeated over several hours—the person eats, vomits, and then eats again—with some patients reporting that they binge and purge up to 20 times during a 24-hour period.

While the binge–purge cycle of behavior is almost always done in secret and accompanied by feelings of self-disgust, shame, and being out of control, some individuals claim they actually have no memory of binge eating and don't really taste the food they consume. Instead, the binge provides a sedative effect, almost as if the food they're eating acts like a tranquilizing drug that helps them calm down and relieve stress. In such cases, it is only when the binge is over that the person experiences feelings of disgust and shame, which they may then try to assuage with the comforting effect of another binge.

> The binge–purge cycle of behavior is almost always done in secret.

The obsessive concern with shape and weight that characterizes anorexia nervosa is also a prominent feature of bulimia nervosa. The following story from Julian, now an adult recovering from bulimia nervosa, illustrates the extent to which such concerns drove him when he was a teen.

"I'd always been somewhat obsessed with how much I weighed and how I looked, I think in part because my mother would often speak negatively about her own body. But in my family, we were also very food-focused. My dad liked to cook elaborate meals, and, as a family, we enjoyed going to new, hip restaurants around town. I never got to the point of starving myself because I loved food too much and couldn't give it up," Julian says. "I pretty much weighed the same thing my whole life but had to work hard not to gain weight. Each day I'd decide what to eat and I usually skipped breakfast or lunch so that I could eat what I wanted for dinner. This routine, which was pretty comfortable for me, started to get messed up when my parents announced they were getting a divorce, and I started to shuttle between different houses." One day, shortly after Julian's parents separated, he realized that he was scheduled to go out to a burger place for lunch with his mom and then to spend the night at his dad's house, where his father would be hosting a dinner party. He went ahead and ate what he considered a "huge" lunch (in this case, a burger and fries). Upon arriving at his dad's house and seeing what he was preparing for dinner, he recalled becoming really upset.

"I thought about what a good cook my dad is and realized there would undoubtedly be lots of irresistible food I couldn't possibly pass up," Julian says. "Thinking I couldn't eat two big meals in one day," Julian got what he "considered a brilliant idea: what goes in always comes out, so why not merely help it along?"

That was the day Julian decided to make himself vomit. He found it surprisingly easy to do, and afterward was absolutely euphoric because he felt cleansed and fresh and ready to partake of whatever delicious food his father served at the dinner party. However, the evening became a blur because instead of "just tasting a little of everything," as he had promised himself he'd do, Julian recalled "gobbling up everything in sight."

"While I was eating, it was like I was in a trance. When my dad's friends were talking to me, all I could do was look around to decide what I'd eat next and I later imagined that I was a distracted, disgusting spectacle, hunting down one type of food after another," he says. In hindsight, he now realizes that he really didn't eat much more than anyone else at the table. "Truth be told, I probably ate less than anyone there, but I still hated myself for 'pigging out' and, as soon as everyone left, I excused myself, went to the bathroom, and made myself throw up again." Thus began a pattern of eating and then purging that would continue for years until Julian finally sought treatment at the behest of a concerned college roommate. Though he has abstained from making himself throw up for years, he still has issues revolving around food, sometimes feeling out of control while he eats, and he battles the urge to purge every time he eats more than he thinks he should.

"I still get a little panicked when I'm invited to a dinner party, especially if the host or hostess tells me about all the great food they're going to serve. I guess that's the greatest irony of being bulimic. Because I've basically maintained the same weight over the years, no one ever suspects I have an eating disorder, so they continue to chatter on about food without realizing how much it can torment me."

Julian's story also illustrates the point that, unlike those with anorexia nervosa—when self-starvation eventually gives them away physically no matter how hard they try to hide it—people with bulimia nervosa usually stay close to or within their typical weight range and can appear perfectly healthy. As one parent says, "In most cases, you can't tell if someone has bulimia just by looking at them. You really have to listen to them and pay attention to their behavior." Indeed, bulimia nervosa is often so hard to spot that it can go undetected for years, and, though by our best estimates up to approximately 15% of individuals with bulimia nervosa are men, they are more likely to be misdiagnosed, leading to further delay in treatment. The outward signs and symptoms that parents should watch for in their daughters or sons include the following:

"You can't tell if someone has bulimia just by looking at them."

- Evidence of purging behaviors (e.g., frequent trips to the bathroom after meals, signs of vomiting, discarded laxative or diuretic wrappers)
- Evidence of binge eating, including the disappearance of large amounts of food or the appearance of wrappers or empty containers indicating that a large amount of food has been consumed during a short period of time
- Swelling of the cheeks or around the jaw (due to salivary gland enlargement)
- Calluses or scars on the back of the knuckles or hands from scraping them against front teeth while using fingers to trigger the gag reflex to induce vomiting
- Dental problems, particularly the erosion of dental enamel from the backs of front teeth
- An excessive exercise regime despite bad weather, injury, or illness
- Behavior indicating that weight loss, dieting, and control of food intake have become primary concerns
- Mood swings

Again, these signs do not in themselves confirm a diagnosis of bulimia nervosa, but if your teen's behavior or outward appearance is raising such red flags, it is important that you consult a medical professional immediately about your child's condition, which, as in the case of anorexia nervosa, will likely be assessed according to the criteria of *DSM-5*. The criteria for bulimia nervosa are shown in Table 2.2 and are further discussed in the section, "What Does a *DSM* Diagnosis Mean?" (see pp. 36–47).

Table 2.2 Diagnostic Criteria for Bulimia Nervosa

A. Recurrent episodes of binge eating. An episode of binge eating is characterized by both of the following:

1. Eating, in a discrete period of time (e.g., within any 2-hour period), an amount of food that is definitely larger than what most individuals would eat in a similar period of time and under similar circumstances.

2. A sense of lack of control over eating during the episode (e.g., a feeling that one cannot stop eating or control what or how much one is eating).

B. Recurrent inappropriate compensatory behaviors in order to prevent weight gain, such as self-induced vomiting; misuse of laxatives, diuretics, enemas, or other medications; fasting; or excessive exercise.

C. The binge eating and inappropriate compensatory behaviors both occur, on average, at least once a week for 3 months.

D. Self-evaluation is unduly influenced by body shape and weight.

E. The disturbance does not occur exclusively during episodes of anorexia nervosa.

Source: Reprinted by permission from the *Diagnostic and Statistical Manual of Mental Disorders* (2013). American Psychiatric Association.

Binge-Eating Disorder

"I first suspected that Camilla had some kind of eating problem when I realized that, a day or two after going grocery shopping, we were out of a lot of the food I had bought—pints of ice cream, family-sized bags of chips, cookies, and that kind of thing," explains her mother, Theresa. "I knew Camilla had been sad a lot lately—she had started a new school because we moved, was pretty mad at us about it, and was having a hard time making friends—but I never saw her eat too much or anything like that." When Theresa became a little more vigilant after her trips to supermarket, she realized that the sink was full of dishes first thing in the morning, even though it had been empty when she went to sleep the night before and that, often, food wrappers inexplicably turned up in her daughter's bedroom garbage. "I also realized that some of the new back-to-school outfits I had bought for Camilla looked a little small on her," Theresa adds, "but I had no idea how to talk to her about all of this without making her feel bad."

Binge-eating disorder, introduced as a provisional diagnosis in *DSM-IV*, was formally included in *DSM-5* following substantial research indicating that it is a distinct and serious eating disorder associated with obesity and other major emotional and physical health complications. Though compensatory behaviors, such as self-induced vomiting and laxative misuse, are absent, the eating disturbance is otherwise akin to that seen in bulimia nervosa. During binge eating episodes, people with binge-eating disorder commonly eat faster than usual, until they are very full and when they are not hungry. They also often eat alone because they are ashamed or embarrassed about how much they eat. The experience of binge eating can be very upsetting and is commonly kept secret, as was the case for Camilla. The criteria for binge-eating disorder are outlined in Table 2.3 and are further discussed in the section, "What Does a *DSM* Diagnosis Mean?" (see pp. 36–47).

When Theresa approached her daughter, Camilla became tearful while explaining, "I get sad and bored because I don't have friends to hang out with and eating is kind of comforting, even if I'm not hungry. Once I start eating, I can't really stop myself and, even though I feel pretty bad afterward and promise myself I won't do it again, the next day it'll again feel like the only thing that will make me feel good." Camilla was aware that she was gaining weight as a result of frequent binge eating, stating that this was "a bummer." While some people

Table 2.3 Diagnostic Criteria for Binge-Eating Disorder

A. Recurrent episodes of binge eating. An episode of binge eating is characterized by both of the following:

1. Eating, in a discrete period of time (e.g., within any 2-hour period), an
amount of food that is definitely larger than what most individuals would
eat in a similar period of time and under similar circumstances.

2. A sense of lack of control over eating during the episode (e.g., a feeling
that one cannot stop eating or control what or how much one is eating).

B. The binge-eating episodes are associated with three (or more) of the
following:

1. Eating much more rapidly than normal.
2. Eating until feeling uncomfortably full.
3. Eating large amounts of food when not feeling physically hungry.
4. Eating alone because of feeling embarrassed by how much one is eating.
5. Feeling disgusted with oneself, depressed, or very guilty afterward.

C. Marked distress regarding binge eating is present.

D. The binge eating occurs, on average, at least once a week for 3 months.

E. The binge eating is not associated with the recurrent use of inappropriate
compensatory behavior as in bulimia nervosa and does not occur exclusively
during the course of bulimia nervosa or anorexia nervosa.

Source: Reprinted by permission from the *Diagnostic and Statistical Manual of Mental
Disorders* (2013). American Psychiatric Association.

with binge-eating disorder may feel very concerned about their
body weight or shape, this is neither universal nor required to
meet criteria for the disorder because the experience of one's
body size can be quite variable.

People with binge-eating disorder tend to first present for
treatment well into adulthood, rather than as teenagers. Yet
the onset of loss of control when eating (feeling unable to stop
eating regardless of the amount of food taken in), eating in
response to emotions, or eating in the absence of hunger often
starts in childhood. This discrepancy highlights the common
difficulty of detecting binge eating behaviors and associated

symptoms. The outward signs and symptoms that parents should watch for include the following:

- Evidence of binge eating or eating in secret, including the disappearance of large amounts of food or the appearance of wrappers or empty containers indicating that a large amount of food has been consumed during a short period of time
- Eating again shortly after completion of a full meal (i.e., eating in the absence of hunger)
- Frequent overeating in response to positive or negative emotions or boredom
- Marked weight increase over a short period of time
- Mood swings

The best current estimates are that 1%–2% of all adults in the United States (as many as 4 million Americans) have binge-eating disorder and that it is somewhat more common among females than males. The rates of binge-eating disorder among adolescents appear to be roughly similar. The dramatic increase in obesity among youngsters in recent years (discussed further in Chapter 5 of this book) raises concerns that the rate of binge-eating disorder may have increased.

Avoidant/Restrictive Food Intake Disorder

"Zach was a picky eater from the start," recalls his father, Andrew, "so we were relieved when he came to us during his junior year in high school to tell us that he was starting to think about what college would be like and was getting worried about his eating. The truth is, we had been worried about it for a long time." Over the years, Zach's parents had had many conversations with their pediatrician about his eating. The pediatrician had at various moments been concerned about Zach's not hitting expected gains in height and weight over time based on his growth curve. Andrew and his wife were frustrated by the limited number of foods Zach was willing to eat. His restrictions, which he could not especially explain beyond labeling new foods as "totally disgusting," caused tension in the family, limiting the restaurants where they could comfortably eat and causing arguments with his younger sister who did not want to eat the same foods every day. Andrew remembers, "When Zach was in elementary school—and not so young, but more like 9 or 10 years old—he continued to have full-blown tantrums if we insisted on his trying to expand his pallet. I took him to a feeding specialist once or twice, but he was totally uncooperative, crawling around the doctor's office when I tried to get him to eat a carrot. Basically, I was so exhausted and humiliated as a parent that I dropped it and we just worked around him, feeding him whatever he was willing to eat."

What Zach was "willing to eat" was limited to one particular brand of macaroni and cheese, plain pizza from a single local restaurant, peanut butter sandwiches, two brands of cereal, milk, fruit, and potato chips. Despite his family's reluctant willingness to work around him, Zach's eating behavior interfered significantly in his day-to-day functioning, especially socially. This is a common feature of ARFID, a diagnosis introduced into the feeding and eating disorders section with the publication of *DSM-5*. It is a broad category that encompasses a variety of clinical presentations. The primary characteristic of ARFID is highly restrictive eating that is far more extreme than the picky eating pattern which is a normal passing phase for many kids. In ARFID, the frequency or intensity of dietary restriction results in low weight (or a lack of weight gain or growth in children), medical problems, or, as in Zach's case, significant social difficulty. The criteria for ARFID are outlined in Table 2.4 and are further discussed in the section, "What Does a *DSM* Diagnosis Mean?" (see pp. 36–47).

As a youngster, Zach was frequently unable to eat with his friends on playdates, at birthday parties, or at sleepovers. Unlike his younger sister, he never attended sleepaway summer

Table 2.4 Diagnostic Criteria for Avoidant/Restrictive Food Intake Disorder (ARFID)

A. An eating or feeding disturbance (e.g., apparent lack of interest in eating or food; avoidance based on the sensory characteristics of food; concern about aversive consequences of eating) associated with one (or more) of the following:

1. Significant weight loss (or failure to achieve expected weight gain or faltering growth in children).
2. Significant nutritional deficiency.
3. Dependence on enteral feeding or oral nutritional supplements.
4. Marked interference with psychosocial functioning.

B. The disturbance is not better explained by lack of available food or by an associated culturally sanctioned practice.

C. The eating disturbance does not occur exclusively during the course of anorexia nervosa or bulimia nervosa, and there is no evidence of a disturbance in the way in which one's body weight or shape is experienced.

D. The eating disturbance is not attributable to a concurrent medical condition or not better explained by another mental disorder. When the eating disturbance occurs in the context of another condition or disorder, the severity of the eating disturbance exceeds that routinely associated with the condition or disorder and warrants additional clinical attention.

Source: Reprinted by permission from the *Diagnostic and Statistical Manual of Mental Disorders* (2013). American Psychiatric Association.

camp. In high school, while most of his peers bought lunch at the cafeteria, he continued to bring a packed lunch daily, and always a peanut butter sandwich and potato chips. When Zach approached his father about wanting to work on his eating, he was driven by a desire to start dating, a wish to "go with friends wherever they want for dinner," and fear about how he would adjust to college life, where he knew he was unlikely to be able to make or buy the exact lunch with which he was comfortable. Though he knew there would be even more eating-related social pressures down the road, it was those just on the horizon that motivated him the most to seek out treatment for his eating disorder.

"Zach and I were both surprised to hear this thing get labeled an eating disorder, because Zach has never cared about his weight or size, but," his father elaborates, "we have come to understand that this kind of eating disorder is *not* about being scared of gaining weight or even very concerned with appearance at all. It's a serious problem, all right, but for Zach, it's more about avoiding certain foods because he's decided they are gross."

According to her mother, Dana, Lily's eating behavior was similarly impairing as Zach's, but her avoidance was driven by something different. "When Lily was 13, she got a stomach virus. In the months that followed, she began to have increased difficulty eating a number of foods, eating by herself if we were in a different part of the house, or eating at a friend's house. She was basically terrified of choking or of becoming nauseous," explains Dana. As Lily progressively ate less, her weight dropped, and her growth slowed. She became socially isolated, often skipping school or sleepovers with complaints of stomach pain. "We took her to so many doctors, including GI specialists, but no one could find anything wrong. We tried eliminating foods that could make her nausea symptoms worse, like dairy, but nothing really helped. We were afraid to insist on Lily eating because we were afraid of *causing* an eating disorder; we had no idea that she already had one!" Finally, Lily's pediatrician suggested to Dana that they see an eating disorders specialist to learn about ARFID.

Unlike individuals with anorexia nervosa, those with ARFID may avoid certain foods because of their sensory features, such as texture or color, or because of fears related to the process of eating, such as choking, not due to concerns about getting fat, body shape, or weight. But both conditions are associated with a lot of anxiety and distress around mealtimes.

For Zach and Lily, treatment involved meeting with a therapist and practicing, during the meetings, eating foods that made them nervous. Zach had to experiment with trying new foods and tolerating them, *especially* if it turned out to be a food that he did not like. "It was a pretty interesting process," Andrew elaborates, "for Zach, and for us, to learn more about the real arbitrariness of his food preferences. Eventually, Zach was able to explain to us that he is basically afraid that if he eats a food he doesn't like, that he will never be able to get the taste out of his mouth. And sometimes even the thought of that makes him nauseous, so he's got to tolerate that, too." Lily's sessions involved practicing with foods that might make her feel like she was choking, such as toasted, dry bread or a spoonful of peanut butter without a drink, and inviting nausea and eating anyways, for example by spinning in a chair for 30 seconds and then taking a bite of banana. Her mother Dana recalls, "As Lily faced her fears, we as her parents faced ours. We learned how to coach her through, and how tolerate our own distress when she got scared."

Like many people dealing with ARFID, it was apparent to Zach's parents and Lily's parents that their child's eating was unusual and creating problems. ARFID is much more than just "picky eating," but seeing this clearly can take time. Still, there are several outward signs to distinguish between the two, including

- an extremely limited array of acceptable foods that creates difficulty taking part in age-appropriate social activities
- persistent food refusal for fear of choking or vomiting
- sudden refusal to eat foods that were previously enjoyed
- persistent food refusal due to lack of appetite or interest, but without a medical or psychological reason to explain it
- frequent, slow eating and/or difficulty completing meals
- failure to grow (in stature and weight) or weight loss.

Research on ARFID is still at an early stage, and, at present, there is no good information on its frequency in the general population. However, individuals with ARFID appear to comprise a small but significant minority of children and adolescents who present to pediatricians with an eating problem. Roughly one-third are males, a much higher proportion than for anorexia nervosa and bulimia nervosa. Not surprisingly, weight is generally reduced but is not as low as among individuals with anorexia nervosa. There is substantial heterogeneity in the symptoms: some individuals have long-standing selective eating, some have experienced a relatively recent traumatic event like choking, and some object to the sensory qualities of particular foods.

What Does a *DSM* Diagnosis Mean?

As we have already mentioned, *DSM-5*[1] provides the criteria most widely used by mental health professionals to describe the exact nature of a patient's problem and to assign a diagnosis. Once an accurate diagnosis has been made, it is easier to know what treatments are appropriate and likely to be successful. This is clearly true for purely physical conditions: bacterial pneumonia responds to antibiotics while viral pneumonia does not. And it is no less true of psychiatric disorders—but, with mental illnesses like eating disorders, nailing down the correct diagnosis can be a challenge. The *DSM-5* diagnostic criteria for eating disorders are based on signs and symptoms reported by patients (and/or their families) seeking treatment because of distress over their symptoms or because of medical, psychological, or social impairment resulting from these problems.

There is an important bidirectional relationship between research and *DSM-5*. In order for a disorder to be recognized in *DSM-5*, there has to be enough knowledge about the disorder to provide clinicians with solid guidance about the characteristics, complications, course, and outcome of the disorder; that is the fundamental reason for distinguishing one disorder from another! (Binge-eating disorder is an illustration. Criteria for this disorder were suggested at the time *DSM-IV* was written, but insufficient information was available to permit its being officially recognized, so the criteria were put in

---

[1] You have probably noticed that the fourth and previous editions of *DSM* are indicated by Roman numerals (*DSM-IV*) whereas the fifth edition by an Arabic numeral (*DSM-5*). This change was made in hopes that, over time, modest changes to the diagnostic criteria might be signified by adding a decimal (for example, *DSM-5.1*) before a complete revision is done, leading to *DSM-6*.

an appendix. By the time *DSM-5* was being written, almost 1,000 articles about binge-eating disorder had been published, and this information justified its official recognition.) The existence of agreed-upon criteria for a disorder provides a critical foundation for *new* research by ensuring that the participants in a study of, for example, a new treatment, all have the same disorder. So, if the new treatment works, clinicians will know which patients may benefit.

The most commonly occurring disorders described in the Feeding and Eating Disorders section of *DSM-5* have already been described: anorexia nervosa, bulimia nervosa, binge-eating disorder, and ARFID. However, several other disorders deserve mention. Two are formally recognized and described: *pica* and *rumination disorder*. Pica is the persistent eating of non-nutritive, non-food substances, like eating dirt. Although such behavior is common (and normal) in infants, who often seem ready to put anything in their mouths, after infancy it is abnormal and can cause significant medical problems. Rumination disorder is characterized by the regurgitation of swallowed food which is then spit out or re-chewed and re-swallowed. While rumination is a behavior that can occur in people with an eating disorder, especially anorexia nervosa or bulimia nervosa, it warrants its own diagnosis if the affected individual does not have symptoms of another eating disorder. Pica and rumination disorder are problems that have been recognized for many years, but only a small number of individuals experiencing them present for treatment, suggesting that their frequency in the general population is low.

More common are problems falling into a broad category in *DSM-5* called Other Specified Feeding or Eating Disorders (OSFEDs). This name is intended to be applied to individuals who have a clinically significant eating disorder that gets in the

Table 2.5 Other Specified Feeding and Eating Disorders (OSFED)

Atypical anorexia nervosa	This category describes individuals who have lost a considerable amount of weight and have developed a number of the behavioral and psychological symptoms of anorexia nervosa, but whose weight remains in the normal or above-normal range.
Subthreshold bulimia nervosa and binge-eating disorder (of low frequency and/or limited duration)	The criteria for bulimia nervosa and binge-eating disorder require that the abnormal eating behaviors occur over at least 3 months and, on average, occur at least once a week. These OSFED categories can be applied to the problems of individuals that fall below these thresholds (in other words, these descriptions might be termed subthreshold bulimia nervosa and subthreshold binge-eating disorder).
Purging disorder	This category describes individuals who do not binge eat but purge frequently after eating because of concerns about their weight or shape.
Night eating syndrome	This disorder describes individuals who often consume substantial amounts of food during the night after they have awakened from sleep.

way of day-to-day functioning and leads to significant distress. They are considered "other" simply because relatively little is known about them compared to the formally recognized eating disorders. Additional research is needed to understand their characteristics and complications and how best to define them. Although specific criteria are not provided, *DSM-5* lists five examples of problems that fall into the OSFED category, described in Table 2.5. Here, we describe two cases of atypical anorexia nervosa and a case of purging disorder.

Atypical Anorexia Nervosa

"If I'm being totally honest, I was happy when Hannah started to lose weight over the summer," admits her mother, Carol.

"Her pediatrician had expressed some concern about her weight at her annual physical last spring, kids at school were not always the kindest, and having struggled with being overweight myself, I know what it feels like to believe that you don't fit in. I just wanted Hannah to feel good about herself and good in her own skin. So when she asked me to let her join a gym and decided to become a vegetarian, I thought it was a good sign that she wanted make some different choices."

Within a few months, Carol was thinking quite differently about what her daughter considered better choices. By this point, Hannah was refusing to eat food cooked by her mother, insisting instead on preparing foods herself to carefully monitor their fat content and to be sure no butter was added. Though she had lost to her "goal weight," Hannah was at the high end of the expected weight range for her age and height. She said, "I still feel huge" and decided to aim for an even lower number on the scale. She skipped a chance to spend a weekend at her grandparents' beach house, a previously beloved summer tradition, because she did not want to miss an exercise class, wear a bathing suit, or be tempted to eat her grandmother's homemade pecan pie. She became visibly distressed when served anything of unknown calories and, after a few bites, would push food around her plate rather than eat any more. Hannah was exhibiting signs of atypical anorexia nervosa, a disorder in which individuals experience behavioral and psychological symptoms of classic anorexia nervosa without reaching an objectively low weight.

"It's hard to tell when she crossed a line from health-conscious to obsessed," Carol states. "At some point, though, I checked her Instagram feed and I realized that every recent post or 'like' had to do with appearance, weight loss, or exercise. My kid who had always loved to follow musicians and post adorable pictures of baby animals was now favoring anything tagged #thinspiration and posting pictures of her changing body." As Carol recognized Hannah's increasing single-mindedness and rigidity about weight, food, and exercise, she also felt her daughter slipping away. "A stranger might have looked at Hannah and seen a normal-weight, health-conscious, introverted kid. But Hannah had been a spirited, carefree, hilarious girl. And now she was on edge all the time, isolating herself due to fears of being expected to 'go with the flow.'"

Judith noticed changes in her daughter's personality as well. "As Katherine continued to lose weight, she alternated between being incredibly irritable—usually when we were encouraging her to loosen up with her food rules—or really sullen. A few of her friends on the traveling soccer team even reached out to us because she had stopped eating at the team's pizza dinners after away games and was often sitting by herself instead of with the group." Judith was then contacted by Katherine's soccer coach after she fainted at practice. Though Katherine had told the coach that she had had plenty to eat earlier, her friends contradicted this, saying that Katherine had thrown out her lunch and they had not seen her eat anything at all that day. "The coach really didn't know who to believe because it wasn't like Katherine *looked* like she was starving or anything. Sure, she was noticeably thinner than before, but not the scary skinny you think of with anorexia," Judith adds.

Neither Hannah nor Katherine were "technically" underweight (according to guidelines provided by the Centers for Disease Control and Prevention) when they experienced symptoms of an eating disorder, but they had lost a great deal of weight from what they used to be. In the teen vulnerable to developing an eating disorder, there is no clearly agreed-upon threshold at which weight loss leads into dangerous territory.

Rather, it is when these teens begin exhibiting the effects of inadequate intake that they can be described as having atypical anorexia nervosa. Much less is known about atypical anorexia nervosa than about the fully recognized eating disorders, but the biological consequences described to occur can include a dangerously low heart rate; irregular, light, or absent menstrual periods; changes in thyroid function; and, in some cases, poor bone health. Similar to what is seen in classic anorexia nervosa, psychological symptoms include low mood, increased anxiety (including fear of fat and weight gain), and extreme concern with body shape and/or weight.

The name "atypical anorexia nervosa" was suggested only a few years ago in *DSM-5*, and sufficient time has not yet passed to estimate how common this eating disorder is and to fully describe the characteristics of individuals who have it and precisely how these characteristics compare to those of individuals with typical anorexia nervosa. Nonetheless, at this relatively early stage, it is clear that this disorder is a major source of distress for a significant number of individuals who present to clinicians for treatment.

Purging Disorder

"Georgie was a sensitive kid, and a little impulsive when she got emotional," recalls her father, Thomas, "but I wouldn't say she ever seemed to pay much attention to her weight or her looks until she started college. She came home for Thanksgiving her freshman year at college and her older brothers teased her a little about having put on the 'freshman fifteen.'" Georgie, it turns out, had already been feeling self-conscious about gaining some weight in college. Though her favorite jeans still fit, she didn't like the way she looked in them. Georgie remembers,

"I felt gross and totally out of shape because the dining options at school were limited, I was partying more than in high school, and it was hard to find time to exercise and study." According to Georgie, her new friends were also different from her friends from home, much more focused on appearance and often critical of their own bodies and others' physiques. "There was so much 'fat talk' that it was impossible not to worry what was being said about you when left the room."

"Fat talk," defined as negative comments about one's own or other's body shape or weight, is highly prevalent in Western culture. Studies indicate that it is associated with body dissatisfaction, which is in turn associated with disordered eating and exercise behavior and symptoms of depression and anxiety. Georgie returned to campus after her break determined to lose weight or at least not to keep gaining. "I had a whole plan to exercise and eat better, but once I was back in the school environment, it was just too hard. I did pretty well limiting myself to salad and no carbs at dinner, but I could not get to the gym. And I was starting to rush a sorority, so the partying did not slow down. One night, after I'd had a few beers, I let myself eat some nachos with my friends and then I just excused myself, went to the restroom and made myself throw up. It just kind of came to me as a solution to the problem, and, before I knew it, I was making myself sick anytime I deviated from my diet or if I hadn't been able to exercise that day. It was also an emotional release sometimes, something to do if I felt angry or upset with my friends or myself. At first, it really seemed like such a perfect fix. But over time, it didn't help me feel better or think less about my body—actually, the opposite—and by the time I realized that, I couldn't stop."

Though Georgie was clearly experiencing the symptoms of purging disorder, inducing vomiting after eating small or normal amounts of food and overly worrying about body shape and weight, it would be another several months before Thomas realized there was a problem. "When she was living at home doing a summer internship, I became suspicious. I could hear her getting sick in the bathroom and it was happening too frequently for it to be a stomach bug. Then we took a family vacation and in cramped hotel quarters, she couldn't vomit, and I saw that her cheeks looked really swollen. When I asked her about it, she broke down and admitted the problem."

Georgie's cheeks looked swollen because her parotid glands were enlarged. This is a common consequence of the sudden discontinuation of frequent vomiting experienced by individuals with any type of eating disorder that involves purging (e.g., anorexia nervosa binge–purge subtype, bulimia nervosa, purging disorder). "I was in so much pain," Georgie describes, "and I was so stressed out because I could not be as controlled with my eating while traveling with my dad and brothers, and that was pretty much the only way I could survive without purging."

Less is known about purging disorder than about anorexia nervosa, bulimia nervosa, or binge-eating disorder. We do know that a significant number of people suffer from it over their lifetimes, probably at about the same rate as for anorexia nervosa and bulimia nervosa. They also experience significant depression and anxiety but, somewhat surprisingly, do not seek out treatment as frequently as do individuals with the recognized eating disorders.

Another Word on the DSM

If you have read this far, you will recognize that the *DSM-5* system is complicated and that there are a variety of diagnostic labels with overlapping features. As the person who knows your child best, you can help to ensure that these diagnostic standards are applied appropriately by, first and foremost, providing the most complete information you can to your child's doctor about the signs and symptoms—the red flags—you've seen that led you to worry that he or she may have an eating disorder. When meeting the doctor for the first time, for example, come prepared to answer questions about when these signs began, how often they occur, how long they last, and how severe they seem. If you have them, it can be very helpful to bring information on your child's physical growth, such as a growth curve chart. Others in your child's daily life—teachers, athletic coaches, school counselors, for example—may be able to help you to provide a comprehensive picture by offering their own observations of your child's behavior in class or the school cafeteria or the playing field. Chances are they've seen at least some of the same signs in school that you have at home. Ask them, and together you can gather the kind of information that will help the doctor understand your child's symptoms well enough to arrive at an accurate diagnosis.

Before a final diagnosis is made, a complete medical checkup will likely be recommended to rule out other diseases that could be causing symptoms similar to an eating disorder and to assess if the eating disorder is causing physical problems. Among the general medical conditions that may cause symptoms that may be mistaken for an eating disorder are intestinal problems like inflammatory bowel disease and celiac disease; diabetes; hyperthyroidism (overactive thyroid); neurological conditions, including brain tumors; and chronic diseases or infections. Psychiatric disorders such as serious depression or obsessive-compulsive disorder (OCD) may also be present. These and other psychiatric conditions are discussed later in this chapter, in the section "What Other Conditions Can Coexist with Eating Disorders?" (pp. 63–68).

What's Not in the *DSM*?

A variety of eating behaviors and attitudes occur with some frequency but are not, in and of themselves, considered disorders. The most familiar is dieting. Modern-day dietary practices and ways of thinking about health promote restrictive eating in various forms. Adolescence is a time of life characterized by experimentation, and, for some teens, restrictive dietary practices—such as vegetarianism and veganism—may be a manifestation of identity formation. Teens are also especially influenced by the eating attitudes and practices of their peers and may test out diets they hear about from friends. Overall, while these practices can restrict food choices and become irritating to family members, they are not considered to be disorders. The majority of dieters, teens and adults, abandon their diets after a few weeks. Others apply restrictions flexibly and in a way that does not interfere with physical or psychological well-being. However, in some teens, dietary practices become increasingly rigid and disruptive, marking the transition from diet to disorder.

Orthorexia, a term introduced at the end of the twentieth century, refers to an unhealthy obsession with a food's quality, origins, or preparation. Orthorexia, per se, is not recognized as an eating disorder. But if the food obsessions described as orthorexia result in an inability to maintain a healthy weight or medical problems, a diagnosis of anorexia nervosa or ARFID may apply. If the highly restrictive eating behavior born out of attitudes about healthy eating results in reactive binge eating episodes, a diagnosis of bulimia nervosa or binge-eating disorder may be appropriate (depending on the presence or absence of compensatory purging behavior).

The peak age of onset of type 1 diabetes is during adolescence, and management of the condition, which requires insulin injections, can be very challenging. When newly diagnosed, misuse of insulin can occur for any number of reasons. However, if a teen with type 1 diabetes persists in misusing insulin for the purpose of weight control, this is sometimes referred to as *diabulimia*. Diabulimia can take the form of skipping doses of insulin to lose weight because the body cannot metabolize carbohydrates without insulin or of increasing doses of insulin to compensate for binge eating episodes. Such behavior can be incredibly dangerous medically. It also likely signals being overly worried about body shape or weight. Diabulimia is not its own diagnostic category because there are already two eating disorder diagnoses—anorexia nervosa and bulimia nervosa—that can be used to capture the most extreme constellation of symptoms.

Some medical illnesses are helped by special diets. For example, celiac disease is a gastrointestinal disorder caused by an allergy to gluten, a protein found in wheat and several other grains, and it is treated by following a diet that is free of gluten. Obviously, a person who follows a gluten-free diet because they have celiac disease does not have an eating disorder! But, in recent years, a number of people have gone on gluten-free diets without being tested for celiac disease out of the belief that a gluten-free diet is good even for people without this disease and will produce a range of health benefits, including weight loss. Taken to an extreme, following such a diet may lead to medical problems or to interference with normal social activities and thus meet criteria for an eating disorder.

It is important to emphasize that *obesity* is not considered an eating disorder. The term "obesity" refers to the presence of an excess of body fat, which usually results from higher energy intake (i.e., caloric consumption) relative to expenditure (i.e., physical activity) over many years. The frequency of obesity among children and adolescents in the United States has more than tripled since the 1970s, and obesity now affects almost 1 in 5 youngsters. Obesity is not considered a mental disorder because a range of factors—biological, behavioral, and environmental—that vary across people contribute to its development.

However, one factor that appears to relate to obesity in some, but not all, cases is binge eating. The presence of binge eating in adolescence is associated with overweight in teens and the onset of overweight and/or obesity in adulthood. The experience of binge eating—feeling a loss of control while eating a large amount of food—is more common in adolescent girls than boys, with approximately 2.5% of girls and less than 1% of boys endorsing this behavior. In children, eating with loss of control, regardless of the amount of food consumed, is associated with higher BMI and body fat, as well as the presence of eating-disordered thoughts, attitudes, and behaviors. Of note, obese, overweight, *and* normal weight youth report episodes of loss of control eating and overeating (eating an objectively large amount of food without feeling out of control).

How Common Are Eating Disorders in Adolescents?

Although the symptoms of eating disorders are known to originate primarily in adolescence, research on their frequency (prevalence) among adolescents is limited. Most studies have focused principally on the occurrence of these disorders in adults, but, even for this age group, knowledge is limited regarding how many individuals actually have an eating disorder and who in particular is vulnerable to developing a specific type, such as anorexia nervosa or bulimia nervosa. As mentioned in Chapter 1, however, experts do seem to agree on these statistics: that, at some point during their lives, approximately 1% of women develop anorexia nervosa, about the same number develop bulimia nervosa, and 2–5% develop binge-eating disorder. Among men, the prevalence rates of anorexia nervosa and bulimia nervosa are approximately one-tenth of those observed in women; the risk for binge-eating disorder among men is a bit lower than among women, but not dramatically. The few studies assessing how many adolescents have eating disorders at a given moment arrive at estimates that are, as would be expected, lower than the lifetime rates: 0.1–1.0% for anorexia nervosa and bulimia nervosa and 1–2% for binge-eating disorder among adolescent girls.

> Eating disorders occur in approximately 1% (anorexia nervosa and bulimia nervosa) to 2–5% (binge-eating disorder) of women over their lifetimes.

Some experts have expressed concern that these figures seriously underestimate the magnitude of the problem among adolescents because they focus primarily on those teens who meet the full *DSM* criteria for a diagnosis of anorexia nervosa, bulimia nervosa, or binge-eating disorder. For example, studies focusing on adolescents have found that almost 30% of adolescent girls of average weight believe they are overweight, and more than 10% at least occasionally engage in very unhealthy weight control behaviors, such as taking diet pills or inducing vomiting to control their weight. In addition, because criteria for ARFID were introduced only in 2013, there have as yet been no population-based studies estimating how frequent it is among either adolescents or adults.

What Causes Eating Disorders, and Who Is at Risk?

Despite extensive information about the characteristics of eating disorders, solid knowledge of their actual cause has so far eluded the scientific community. Simply put, no one can tell you, with any scientific certainty, why your child has developed an eating disorder. Still, because of the obvious importance of the question, investigators are urgently committed to uncover information about these disorders that could shed light on their causes and ultimately improve their treatment and prevention. In this section, we'll first explain why identifying the causes of eating disorders is so challenging and then focus on several factors (including those currently under investigation by researchers) that may contribute to the risk of developing an eating disorder.

> No one can tell you, with any scientific certainty, why your child has developed an eating disorder.

If there was a simple, straightforward, and single cause for eating disorders, how would we recognize it? We'd expect that it would be found in all people who developed an eating disorder, that the cause would be present *before* the disorder began, and that the cause would not be found among people without the illness. An example of a simple relationship between a cause and an illness is AIDS. A virus, called HIV, causes AIDS: AIDS only develops among people who have contracted

HIV, and people who do not have HIV do not develop AIDS. The causes of psychiatric illnesses, including eating disorders, are much more complicated. It does not appear that eating disorders have a single cause; rather, multiple influences, called *risk factors*, seem to combine and interact to eventually result in the occurrence of an eating disorder. As we will discuss, some of these risk factors appear to be an individual's personal characteristics, like his or her gender, and others appear to be in the world around the individual, like the culture in which he or she grows up. Because so many factors seem possibly to have an influence, it has been very difficult for researchers to sort out which ones are most significant.

Part of the problem in identifying the important risk factors is that eating disorders, especially full-blown disorders, are not very common. As we described in the last section, only a small percent of young people will ever develop an eating disorder that meets *DSM-5* criteria. This poses a real challenge for researchers. If eating disorders are caused by the interaction of multiple causes, each of which increases the chances by a small amount, a study to prove these risk factors were really important would have to follow thousands of young people for many years, from before the eating disorders developed until early adulthood, when all the people who were going to develop an eating disorder would have been identified. The scientific and financial requirements for such a study are daunting, and, to date, no large study of this type has been done.

What researchers have identified are *possible* risk factors— biological, environmental, social, and psychological phenomena that appear to increase the likelihood that an adolescent will develop either eating disorder symptoms or a full-blown syndrome. A large number of such risk factors have been described, but the scientific evidence supporting many of them is far from overwhelming. In the next section, we describe several risk factors about which some information is available and which may help you to think through why your child might be more likely to have a problem.

GENDER

Although, as previously mentioned, males are not immune from eating disorders, being female is the most obvious and reliable risk factor for the development of several of the eating disorders, especially anorexia nervosa and bulimia nervosa: about 90% of individuals with these disorders are female. Many theories ranging from the sociocultural to the biological have been offered for this phenomenon, but no conclusive explanation has yet been found as to why, consistently across various cultures, more females than males develop anorexia nervosa and bulimia nervosa.

The effect of gender is not as strong for binge-eating disorder: males make up about one-third of individuals with binge-eating disorder. And, although research on ARFID is at an early stage, it appears that males constitute at least a substantial minority of individuals with this disorder.

In recent years, evidence has emerged suggesting that sexual minorities (e.g., gay, lesbian, bisexual individuals), including transgender individuals, are at increased risk for the development of disordered eating and of eating disorders. Investigators speculate that this may be due to increased focus on physical attributes and to high levels of victimization and discrimination.

PUBERTY

Although the onset of eating disorders can occur at any time throughout the life span, the greatest risk period for the onset of anorexia nervosa, bulimia nervosa, and binge-eating disorder is around the time of and just following puberty. As is true with gender, there is no real certainty about why the onset of puberty increases risk, but again, theories ranging from the sociocultural (girls may be more vulnerable during puberty to social pressures to be thin, particularly in the context of their bodily changes, such as increases in fat stores) to the biological (hormonal changes that can trigger other biological processes) have been suggested. ARFID, on the other hand, appears often to develop during childhood.

> The greatest risk period for the onset of anorexia nervosa, bulimia nervosa, and binge-eating disorder is around the time of puberty.

The Brain

Since eating disorders are defined by the occurrence of abnormal eating behavior and since behavior is controlled by the brain, there must be something(s) amiss in the brains of individuals with eating disorders, and, presumably the brain-based abnormalities must vary across the different eating disorders. Unfortunately, despite decades of research by numerous researchers, it has proved difficult to get far beyond these largely self-evident statements.

Much scientific work in the 1990s and the early years of this century focused on *neurotransmitters*, the chemicals used by nerve cells in the brain to communicate with one another. In particular, there is evidence suggesting that some eating disorders may be associated with changes in the brain's serotonin system. One of a number of neurotransmitters, *serotonin* is involved in the regulation of many normal phenomena, including both mood and behavior, such as eating. But, although there is good circumstantial evidence that the serotonin system of individuals with eating disorders is not entirely normal, exactly what is wrong with it is not clear. Furthermore, it is very difficult to sort out the "cart or horse" issue: Do abnormalities in the serotonin system precede the development of the eating disorder and increase the risk? Or are the abnormalities only another of the many physical changes that result from disturbances in weight and eating behavior?

In the past decade, investigators have increasingly applied insights and techniques from the field of cognitive neuroscience to probe eating disorders. *Cognitive neuroscience* is concerned with the brain processes that underlie thinking and behavior and is particularly focused on the neural connections, or circuits, within the brain. This type of research often uses computerized tasks that require participants to make decisions in a complicated and changing environment and can thereby assess how different people approach problems. Such tasks can be combined with sophisticated brain-imaging techniques, especially *functional MRI* (fMRI), which measures brain activity by detecting changes associated with blood flow, to see what brain circuits are engaged.

In the past several years, our group at Columbia has used this approach to understand the restrictive eating behavior that is characteristic not only of anorexia nervosa but also of bulimia nervosa when individuals with that disorder are not engaged in binge eating. In collaboration with sophisticated cognitive neuroscientists, we have developed a computerized task that presents participants with images of foods and asks them to make choices, in terms of what they would like to eat, between a neutral "reference" food and a range of low- and high-fat foods. Not surprisingly, individuals with anorexia nervosa consistently avoid choosing the high-fat foods, as do individuals with bulimia nervosa when they are not engaged in binge eating. What is surprising, and we believe important, is that people with anorexia nervosa use a different part of their brain—the dorsal striatum—when making decisions about what to eat compared with people without an eating disorder.

The *dorsal striatum*, a structure deep in the middle of the brain, becomes active when someone engages in a very well-practiced, and therefore automatic, behavior. Our theory is that, as individuals with anorexia nervosa, over a long period of time, continue to decide to avoid high-fat foods, such decisions become more automatic and entrenched and that the increased activity in the dorsal striatum reflects that change.

Studies of individuals with bulimia nervosa have suggested that, when shown pictures of appealing foods, the brain shows an enhanced response, consistent with increased brain reactivity to foods individuals are more likely to consume during episodes of binge-eating. Neuroscientific research is also currently underway in individuals with ARFID.

GENETICS

Studies have demonstrated that relatives of those with eating disorders are at greater risk of developing an eating disorder themselves. Although this may be due in part to the family environment, there is very strong evidence that genes affect the risk of developing an eating disorder and therefore play a major role in determining why eating disorders occur more frequently in some families.

> There is good evidence that eating disorders tend to run in families.

But despite the compelling evidence that genetic influences contribute to an individual's vulnerability to develop an eating disorder, no single gene or set of genes makes it inevitable that someone will develop an eating disorder. In other words, specific genes increase (or decrease) the chances of someone developing an eating disorder, but only by a little. Furthermore, the impact of genes on the risk of developing an eating disorder is dependent on a complex interaction between the individual's genetic makeup and their environment. The same holds true for other complex, multifaceted disorders like obesity, schizophrenia, and high blood pressure.

SOCIOCULTURAL FACTORS: THE "THIN IDEAL" AND THE ROLE OF THE MEDIA

The emphasis on thinness—and more generally, on an individual's weight and body shape as measures of personal worth—is pervasive in our society, and, indeed, weight concerns and dieting are the norm in the United States and other developed countries. Does this cultural phenomenon necessarily predispose one to acquiring an eating disorder? Of all the possible risk factors to be implicated in the onset of these disorders, this one—the predominantly Western cultural ideal of thinness—may be the most familiar to the public because of the persistent presentation of images of thin, attractive, and successful young people in the mass media. Donna, whose daughter Chelsey was diagnosed with anorexia nervosa at age 16, has much to say on this very point.

"Our culture equates success and beauty and popularity with a thin body. Because those skin-and-bones actresses, models, and singers are highly successful, they also become role models for our children. And now there are also reality TV types and teen and young adult 'influencers' who specifically aim to influence our kids. For heaven's sake, they're *stars* and every magazine you pick up has one of them on the cover.

Then, inside the magazine, there are tons of ads about dieting and losing weight. On TV it's the same thing. Online,
social media allows all kinds of people to become mini-celebs
through their blogs and Instagram, Twitter, and Facebook following. Content—provocative selfies, articles on the latest
'clean eating' trend, YouTube videos—is suggested based on
your Internet search history and pop-up ads claim that if you
just buy a certain diet book or diet pill, you, too, can be as thin
and happy as that movie star. It's appalling that positive things
are attributed to having a thin body. But how can we expect
our children to see themselves for who and what they are when
they are continually bombarded with all these images?"

The fact that eating disorders are described primarily in
developed countries does suggest that media-driven Western
cultural influences, particularly the "thin ideal," are somehow involved in their onset, but precisely how this may be so
remains unclear. Social media, which has exploded in popularity in the past decade, differs from traditional forms of media
by allowing users to create their own content that is then subject to feedback from others, and vice versa. This means that,
in addition to comparisons with celebrities and celeb-type
"influencers," teens (and adults) have increased opportunity
to engage in unhelpful comparisons with a much wider swath
of friends and acquaintances. In general, time spent on social
networking sites is associated with body image distress and
disordered eating. The use of appearance-related features, such
as posting or viewing photographs, is correlated with internalization of the thin ideal and body image disturbance, and,
among adolescent girls specifically, selfie-taking and a preoccupation with curating an online persona is correlated with
increased risk of eating disorder symptoms. However, even in
industrialized countries, where exposure to the thin ideal and

dieting either through traditional or new media platforms is nearly universal, where dissatisfaction with the size and shape of one's own body is chronic, especially in women, and where the overwhelming majority of women say they would like to lose weight, only a very small number of young women actually develop clinically significant eating disorders. For those vulnerable individuals, social media networks provide a readily accessible forum for the exchange of potentially dangerous, illness-related information. In fact, there are websites that are devoted to providing information and instruction on unhealthy methods of weight control.

"Time spent on social networking sites is associated with body image distress and disordered eating."

The incidence of eating disorders elsewhere in the world suggests that the illnesses are not confined to areas that embrace the Western ideal of slimness. While the Western cultural imperative to be thin in order to be attractive may, indeed, increase the chances that one will develop an eating disorder, other factors must certainly also be important.

RACE AND SOCIOECONOMIC STATUS

Traditionally, eating disorders were thought to affect primarily white women from higher socioeconomic classes. However, no race or ethnicity is immune and each of the six formally defined eating disorders has been described among individuals of all racial and socioeconomic groups. There continue to be hints that different ethnic groups may be more or less vulnerable to developing specific disorders. For example, it appears that anorexia nervosa occurs less frequently among African Americans and that binge-eating disorder may be somewhat more common among Latino Americans. Ongoing cross-cultural research seeks to refine such findings and to understand them, including by examining sociocultural influences that may differentially impact vulnerability across groups.

Within the United States, although anorexia nervosa still tends to occur more among the financially better off, generally, feeding and eating disorders are broadly distributed across socioeconomic categories. Of more than 300 health conditions evaluated in a Global Burden of Disease Study, anorexia nervosa and bulimia nervosa rank as the 12th leading contributor to health burdens in high-income countries and 46th in low- and middle-income countries. This underscores their impact across the socioeconomic spectrum worldwide.

> "Each of the six formally defined eating disorders has been described among individuals of all racial and socio-economic groups."

PERSONALITY TRAITS

A number of studies suggest that personality characteristics such as negative self-evaluation, low self-esteem, obsessiveness, and perfectionism may be linked to the development of anorexia nervosa and bulimia nervosa. Some studies have focused on recovered individuals and have presumed that traits persisting after recovery represent enduring traits that preceded the onset of the disorder. However, it is clear that psychological and emotional traits that are commonly viewed as enduring features of someone's personality can be seriously distorted by the presence of an eating disorder, and it is possible that, even after recovery, some personality traits may be persistent after-effects of having had the disorder.

DIETING

Dieting is one of the most talked-about possible risk factors for eating disorders and yet one of the least well characterized. Part of the problem is with terminology. The term "dieting" itself is complex, laden with many meanings, and is used to refer to a variety of attitudes and behaviors. At its most basic, the word "diet" means simply "habitual nutrition"—that is, what we ordinarily eat and drink to live day to day. A "special diet" might be one in which certain foods are off limits—say, because they cause an allergic reaction, or because they raise cholesterol, or because they're prohibited by one's religion. And then there's the type of diet one goes on in order to gain or, more often, to lose weight.

It is, of course, in the sense of losing weight that most people use the term. In 2000, the National Task Force on the Prevention and Treatment of Obesity defined *dieting* as "the intentional and sustained restriction of caloric intake for the purposes of reducing body weight or changing body shape, resulting in a significant negative energy balance." This implies that, strictly speaking, dieting should only be called "dieting" if it is associated with weight loss. From this perspective, attempts to restrict caloric intake that do not result in weight loss represent unsuccessful dieting, and it is important to note that such attempts are frequently described by individuals with symptoms of eating disorders. Unfortunately, though, the literature on eating disorders does not distinguish between successful and unsuccessful attempts to restrict caloric intake, making it difficult to determine whether successful and unsuccessful dieting play similar roles in the development of eating disorders.

Other terms complicate the literature as well. *Restrained eating* and *dietary restraint,* for example, are frequently used in discussions of risk factors for the development and maintenance of eating disorders. Dietary restraint, a frame of mind linked with the attempt to diet, tends to be associated with unsuccessful dieting, but both it and *restrained eating* are used to describe a range of attitudes and behaviors, including food avoidance.

In part because of these terminological issues, the research on the relationship between dieting and eating disorders is confusing and does not resolve the degree to which the "dieting" commonly engaged in by large numbers of young women should be considered a major risk factor for the development of eating disorders. What may be a clearer distinction, however, is the difference between (1) dieting and (2) *unhealthy weight-loss behaviors*—that is, activities that are associated with some risk of physical harm, such as self-induced vomiting, laxative and diet pill abuse, complete food avoidance for extended periods of time (fasting), and excessive exercise to lose weight. These types of behavior *are* relevant in discussions of risk factors for eating disorders because a considerable number of young people engage in these practices, and it is likely that these behaviors are, for many individuals, the beginning of the development of an eating disorder meeting full *DSM-5* criteria.

> The research on the relationship between dieting and eating disorders is inconclusive.

ACTIVITIES WITH A FOCUS ON BODY SHAPE AND WEIGHT
Activities that emphasize weight and appearance (e.g., ballet, gymnastics, wrestling, figure skating, distance running) have been investigated as risk factors for the development of anorexia nervosa and bulimia nervosa. Elite athletes and ballet

dancers have been found to have an increased prevalence of both diagnosable eating disorders and disordered eating symptoms, with a prevalence of *DSM-5* anorexia nervosa that is 4 to 25 times higher among ballet dancers than in the general population. Models, actresses, entertainers, and others whose appearance plays a major role in their careers are also likely to be at a higher risk for developing an eating disorder. But even here, cause and effect are hard to separate as it may be that the athletic and artistic worlds attract individuals who are already preoccupied with shape and weight or had other risk factors that contribute both to their choice of a career and to the emergence of an eating disorder.

> "Elite athletes and ballet dancers . . . have an increased prevalence of both diagnosable eating disorders and disordered eating symptoms."

FAMILY RELATIONSHIPS

In the 1950s, when the occurrence of virtually all emotional problems was explained on the basis of theories from psychoanalysis, it was widely believed that particular patterns of family interaction, especially early in life, were causative factors in the development of eating disorders. These ideas were never confirmed scientifically, and investigators are currently much more cautious about ascribing the risk of eating disorders to the family environment. There is often dysfunction in the family when a child has an eating disorder. But it is very hard to know whether such family problems have any role in the development of the disorder or whether they are simply manifestations of distress about an ill child in an otherwise normally functioning family.

Peer Influence

Adolescence is a developmental stage during which a child's individuation from the family intensifies as his or her attention shifts increasingly toward peers, and the friends made in these formative years can be influential for the decades to follow. Personality variables play a significant role in peer selection. Insecurity about appearance and the importance of achieving the thin ideal can therefore get magnified within certain groups of friends. In adolescent girls, longitudinal research has found that exposure to friends who are dieting predicts greater body dissatisfaction, use of extreme and unhealthy weight control behaviors, and loss of control eating at 5-year follow-up. Conversely, a peer group that does not overly value weight, body shape, or dieting practices may help protect a vulnerable teen from extreme internalization of the thin ideal.

"Friends made in these formative years can be influential for the decades to follow."

In college samples, roommate dieting frequency has been found to predict an individual's drive for thinness, bulimic symptoms, and purging status. Roommate dieting frequency is also associated with the likelihood of unhealthy weight control behaviors for women in their 30s, despite the changes in social environments that are likely to occur over time. Essentially, it appears that peers form a micro-environment that can contribute to or protect against eating-disordered thoughts and behaviors. Exactly how much (and by what mechanism) a "contagion" effect plays a role in eating disturbances—particularly in shared living environments such as dorms, apartments, or sorority/fraternity houses—remains an important area of study.

(Further attention to peer influence or support in the maintenance of eating disorders is given in Chapter 5).

CHILDHOOD TRAUMA

Much has been written in the popular media about the role of childhood trauma, and particularly sexual abuse, in the development of eating disorders. Although there are significant limitations to our knowledge, research studies have found that individuals with eating disorders are, indeed, more likely to report histories of such traumatic experiences than those without the disorders. However, there are two additional important findings. First, among individuals with eating disorders, only a minority appear to report such histories. By no means can one conclude that because a young woman has developed an eating disorder, she must have been abused as a child. Second, the occurrence of childhood trauma increases one's chances of developing *many* emotional and behavioral problems, so such trauma is probably best viewed as a nonspecific risk factor for a range of problems later in life.

What Other Conditions Can Coexist with Eating Disorders?

Unfortunately, many adolescents with eating disorders struggle with other emotional, behavioral, and psychological problems as well. In fact, across all age groups, more than 70% of those with anorexia nervosa and about 75% of those with bulimia nervosa and binge-eating disorder are affected by them. As ARFID is relatively new to the category of feeding and eating disorders, less is known about its co-occurrence with other problems. However, initial reports suggest a low overlap with mood disorders, a modest overlap with obsessive-compulsive disorder (OCD), and a more robust overlap with other anxiety disorders and autism spectrum disorders. Whether these problems—called *comorbidities* by health professionals—are possible causes or consequences of the eating disorder is difficult to determine, but what is clear is that their existence can complicate or delay the diagnosis and treatment of the eating disorder. Valerie illustrates this point with the following story.

"At age 14, our daughter suddenly showed very little interest in her personal appearance. She started wearing baggy hoodie sweatshirts, mostly dark colors, spent large amounts of time in her room by herself with the door closed, and had no interest in joining us or her friends for activities that had always been important to her. She wasn't sleeping well either. We didn't know what was wrong. We wondered if she'd started smoking marijuana, since we knew her older brother did so sometimes, or had a major fight with her friends or something. That was not the case. This was actually the first sign of depression. We recently found out that chronic depression and anorexia go hand-in-hand for many patients."

"Our daughter had dual problems that took years to diagnose. We did not have any prior knowledge of eating disorders. After we knew she was underweight, we still faced a medical community that had no idea what to do for her first. She was in and out of facilities to treat the depression for years before we came to understand that her low weight, her eating disorder, was part of the reason for her low mood and probably why the medications she had tried were not working."

Valerie's frustration with the difficulties in recognizing and treating her daughter's coexisting illnesses is understandable. Unfortunately, other emotional, behavioral, and psychological disorders often share symptoms similar to those of eating disorders, which can often make diagnosis difficult.

Other emotional, behavioral, and psychological disorders often share symptoms similar to those of eating disorders.

Other disorders that commonly occur with eating disorders are the following:

- *Mood disorders.* Significant mood disturbances, termed "affective disorders" by mental health professionals, commonly co-occur with anorexia nervosa and bulimia nervosa. In particular, many individuals with eating disorders also suffer from major depressive disorder. According to the *DSM-5,* major depression essentially involves either being depressed or irritable nearly all the time or losing interest or enjoyment in almost everything. It is not just a passing case of the blues, nor is it a sign of personal weakness, nor can it simply be wished away. It lasts for at least 2 weeks and is associated with other symptoms, such as a change in eating or sleeping habits, lack of energy, feelings of worthlessness, trouble with concentration, or thoughts of suicide. Affective disorders like major depression may begin before or after the onset of eating disorders, or the disorders can begin at the same time. It's important to know that substantial weight loss as occurs in anorexia nervosa can, by itself, produce many of the symptoms of depression, and, during treatment, as weight returns to normal, these symptoms improve or disappear.

- *Anxiety disorders.* People with anxiety disorders suffer from exaggerated worry and tension, even when there is little to worry about. Symptoms can manifest themselves physically as well as emotionally. The anxiety disorder that most frequently predates the onset of anorexia nervosa or bulimia nervosa is *social phobia* (excessive self-consciousness in social situations). The rate of lifetime co-occurrence between anxiety disorders and binge-eating disorder is estimated to be between one-half to two-thirds, with specific phobia and social phobia being the two most common. Early research on ARFID suggests that a substantial proportion of individuals with ARFID also describe problems with anxiety.

- *OCD.* People with OCD experience unwanted, recurrent thoughts, feelings, ideas, or sensations (i.e., obsessions) and feel compelled by an urgent need to engage in certain rituals (often to get rid of or prevent obsessions). The link between OCD and anorexia nervosa is especially compelling because of similarities between the two conditions (namely, the presence of obsessional thought patterns and stereotyped behaviors), and OCD is known to pre-date anorexia nervosa in some cases. Rates of OCD are somewhat elevated among people with bulimia nervosa as well.

- *Substance use disorders.* Individuals with eating disorders marked by binge eating behaviors, including binge-eating disorder, bulimia nervosa, and those with the binge–purge subtype of anorexia nervosa, have an increased tendency to engage in problematic substance use behavior, such as the abuse of alcohol, cocaine, and marijuana. In both anorexia nervosa and bulimia nervosa, substance abuse tends to begin after the onset of the eating disorder.

- *Autism spectrum disorder.* Individuals with autism spectrum disorder often exhibit idiosyncrasies around eating and may be quite selective in what they are willing to consume. When the eating is especially problematic, they may receive a diagnosis of ARFID.

• *Personality disorders.* Defined as a constellation of personality traits that significantly impair one's ability to function socially or cause personal distress, personality disorders are considered by some researchers to be a significant comorbidity with eating disorders. Among the personality disorders that may occur with anorexia nervosa, for example, is avoidant personality disorder, which is characterized by hypersensitivity to rejection and criticism, low self-esteem, and social withdrawal; however, as is the case with symptoms of depression, starvation itself leads to social withdrawal and other symptoms that may seem like the individual's personality has changed. A typical comorbidity associated with bulimia nervosa is *borderline personality disorder*, which is marked by impulsivity, intense or chaotic interpersonal relationships, unstable self-image, and extreme emotions, such as intense and inappropriate anger. However, especially in adolescents, it can be very difficult to sort out whether such symptoms are manifestations of an eating disorder, which will subside if the eating disorder is successfully treated, or whether they indicate the existence of a personality disorder. In any case, because so many psychological changes occur during adolescence, most mental health professionals are reluctant to apply the diagnosis of a personality disorder to individuals under the age of 18.

Another phenomenon that can complicate the diagnosis of eating disorders is something that mental health professionals call *diagnostic migration*, or the movement of an individual's condition across diagnostic categories from one eating disorder or subtype to another. For example, as indicated in Table 2.1 (p. 38), in *DSM-5*, there are two subtypes of anorexia nervosa. Everyone with anorexia nervosa severely restricts how much they eat, but about half of those with anorexia nervosa, although they severely restrict their food intake almost all the time, occasionally engage in episodes of overeating, and many of these individuals induce vomiting following such episodes. (Even though such behavior occurs in bulimia nervosa, these individuals receive a diagnosis of anorexia nervosa because they are underweight.) A frequent pattern of diagnostic migration is from the restricting subtype of anorexia nervosa to the binge–purge subtype, reflecting the development of bulimic symptoms; this change tends to occur within the first few years after the development of anorexia nervosa. Many of these individuals gain weight in association with the binge eating, leading to a change in diagnosis from anorexia nervosa to bulimia nervosa. Transitions from a diagnosis of bulimia nervosa to another eating disorder are less common, but a small number of individuals will lose significant weight, requiring a change in their diagnosis from bulimia nervosa to the binge–purge subtype of anorexia nervosa. A smaller number stop purging but continue to binge eat, so their diagnosis changes to binge-eating disorder. Precisely what factors lead to these transitions and why they occur in some people but not others are unclear.

The Dangers of Doing Nothing

"After Jody admitted to me that she was bulimic," Shirley says, "I immediately went straight to Google. I found some good educational resources, but it was a little hard to know which sites to trust. I also found a bunch of books online, but they were all different. Some were memoirs, others were workbooks, and others still were textbooks for professionals. I tried to stick with the material meant for parents. What I read gave me a bit of insight, but I did not realize at the time that I could not hear what I could not hear. My denial, misconceptions, and misunderstandings about the illness caused me to ignore information that I blithely assumed applied to other people with disordered eating."

Dana had a hard time finding much information about Lily's ARFID diagnosis at all. "It was really frustrating. When we finally had the problem clearly identified, there wasn't much more to learn before jumping into the treatment being recommended. Lily's doctors explained that this was a relatively new diagnosis, so we could read about eating disorders in general and about exposure therapy for anxiety disorders, but we would have to cobble things together and be very active in asking our questions directly to her treatment team. I felt so grateful that we had found our way to a team of specialists. I really hope that in a few years it'll be different, that there will be more that's written about ARFID so that parents everywhere can have access to good information."

Though Shirley had more information at her disposal about her daughter's disorder, there were still bumps in the road. "Jody also insisted that we not tell anyone—she would determine when and to whom her bulimia was revealed. We told ourselves we were honoring her wishes. I can no longer tell myself that lie. I was as ashamed as Jody was to acknowledge her behavior, and I liked the *results* of her behavior nearly as much as she did—what a trim and pretty daughter I had— such hubris, such ignorance, such humanness. Our silence assured a feeling of isolation in my fears for my daughter, and denial prevented all of us from understanding a lot."

"Denial prevented all of us from understanding a lot."

Diane echoes similar sentiments regarding her son Michael's struggle with anorexia nervosa. "I knew there were problems, but when he insisted ongoing on a 3-week backpacking trip with his college friends during the summer, I only agreed because he promised he would eat." By the time Michael got back from the backpacking trip, however, he'd lost another 15 pounds. "The summer was nearly over, and we were frantically trying to figure out what to do because he only had 3 weeks before the start of the next semester. The best advice I can offer to other parents is to not stick your head in the ground. Don't think it's a phase that will go away. Follow your gut reactions and, if you're worried, do something about it. Even if your kid is in college and supposed to be more independent. When it comes to an eating disorder, it's better for you to be chastised for being an overinvolved alarmist than it is to let your kid to keep getting sicker because his eating disorder isn't being treated."

> "Don't think it's a phase that will go away. Follow your gut reactions and, if you're worried, do something about it."

Exactly so. Faced with the prospect that your child has an eating disorder, your initial reactions may be alarm, disbelief, denial, confusion, anger, bewilderment—in short, a barrage of very powerful feelings, and perhaps even guilt that you're somehow responsible for the condition. But with all the feelings that you must contend with at this time, it is critically important that you not let them overwhelm or paralyze you. These disorders are complex and can happen in any family. They occur for reasons that are unknown but that likely involve factors beyond anyone's conscious control. What *is* in your control as a parent, though, is how you deal with the situation now. Confronted with the visible signs or red flags that your child has a serious problem, you can take charge, face the problem head on, and act in your child's best interests by seeking medical help immediately, just as you would if your child had a serious, purely physical illness. To do otherwise— as Diane says, to "stick your head in the ground"—is to risk facing more serious problems down the road.

Medical Complications of Eating Disorders

Eating disorders are associated with serious medical complications and can be fatal. Most of the complications result from malnutrition or occur as a result of unhealthy weight-control behaviors, like vomiting. Even adolescents who do not meet full *DSM-5* criteria for an eating disorder but have significant symptoms may be at risk of developing these complications. Serious though they can be, almost all the complications are reversible with nutritional rehabilitation and symptom improvement. However, in an adolescent whose growth and development are not yet complete, the medical consequences of eating disorders can be long-lasting and irreversible. Particularly worrisome complications for adolescents include growth retardation, pubertal delay or arrest, and impaired strengthening of bone.

MEDICAL COMPLICATIONS OF ANOREXIA NERVOSA

The most important medical complications of anorexia nervosa result from malnutrition. Muscle wastes, cheeks are sunken, and bones protrude through the skin, which itself may be pale, dry, and yellow in color. Body temperature is usually low, and the individual's hands and feet may be cold and blue; he or she will often need multiple layers of clothing to keep warm. Fine downy hair (lanugo) may be present over the arms, back, and face. Scalp hair is dry, listless, and brittle, and there may be evidence of hair loss. Resting pulse and blood pressure are both low—for example, the pulse may be as low as 30 to 40 beats per minute, in contrast to the normal average of between 60 and 100 beats per minute—and changes in both pulse and blood pressure, such as when the person stands up, may cause dizziness or fainting.

Malnutrition can lead to life-threatening deterioration in the functioning of the heart and cardiovascular system. The effects of malnutrition are often aggravated by imbalances of electrolytes in the bloodstream; electrolytes are minerals like sodium and potassium needed to maintain physical functions, such as heart rhythm, muscle contraction, and brain function. An electrolyte imbalance is more likely to occur in those who are vomiting or abusing laxatives or diuretics. Individuals who drink excessive amounts of water, either to defray hunger or to falsely elevate body weight before a medical visit, risk low sodium levels in the blood (called *hyponatremia*), which can lead to seizures, coma, and even death caused by "water intoxication."

Medical complications such as congestive heart failure can occur during the early phases of refeeding, particularly if weight is extremely low. Bloating and constipation are frequent complaints of patients with anorexia nervosa, indicating delayed gastric emptying and decreased intestinal functioning. Malnutrition also causes the metabolism to slow down, requiring fewer calories to function. Suppression of the bone marrow often occurs, resulting in low white blood cell, red blood cell, and platelet counts. Despite the low white blood cell count, there does not appear to be an increased risk of infection unless a person is severely underweight. The major neurological complications of eating disorders are seizures and cerebral atrophy (a reduction in the size of the brain), as well as impairment of attention, concentration, and memory. In addition, the level of glucose in the blood can drop to a dangerously low level (a condition called *hypoglycemia*) and produce confusion and seizures.

The occurrence of anorexia nervosa prior to the completion of an individual's growth interferes with bone development, and some adolescents may never reach their full height. The delay in bone growth is more likely to occur in adolescent boys than in girls because the growth spurt of boys occurs later and lasts longer than that of girls, whose growth is almost complete by their first menstruation (usually around age 12). In both boys and girls, anorexia nervosa disrupts the hormonal changes that are a normal part of puberty. For example, as we mentioned previously, loss of menstruation, or *amenorrhea*, is a cardinal feature of anorexia nervosa among girls. Pituitary and ovarian hormones controlling menstruation are all low, and the uterus and ovaries shrink in size. If weight is restored and the girl's menstrual periods resume, however, the ability to conceive should be normal.

Loss of menstruation, or amenorrhea, is a cardinal feature of anorexia nervosa among girls.

A serious side effect of prolonged amenorrhea and a low estrogen state is reduced bone mineral density, a substantial reduction in the strength of bones. It is related to poor nutrition, low body weight, estrogen deficiency, and high levels of cortisol (a hormone released by the adrenal glands that is responsible for many of the physiological effects of stress) in the bloodstream. The reduction in bone density in females with anorexia nervosa is more severe than it is in those with other conditions associated with amenorrhea and a low estrogen state, suggesting that, in addition to estrogen deficiency, nutritional factors play an important role.

Adolescence is a critical time for bone mass acquisition. Whether or not a young woman will develop osteoporosis in later life depends not only on the rate of bone loss in adulthood—a normal accompaniment of aging—but also on the amount of bone present at skeletal maturity, often referred to as *peak bone mass*. Many studies have shown that peak bone mass is achieved toward the end of adolescence. A woman who develops anorexia nervosa during adolescence may not reach a normal peak bone mass, placing her at increased risk of developing fractures. This risk may persist for years after recovery from the disorder.

It must also be reiterated that anorexia nervosa has one of the highest mortality rates among psychiatric disorders. The most common causes of death among patients struggling with the disorder are the effects of starvation and suicide. The suicide rate among women with anorexia nervosa is approximately 20 times higher than for women of a similar age in the general population.

Medical Complications of Bulimia Nervosa

Bulimic behaviors, such as self-induced vomiting and laxative and diuretic abuse, can lead directly to dehydration and electrolyte disturbances. Indirectly, they can also cause water retention when these inappropriate behaviors abruptly cease and the body "overcompensates" by temporarily hanging on to extra water.

A reduced level of potassium in the blood (*hypokalemia*) is the most common electrolyte disturbance found in patients who vomit, use laxatives, or take diuretics. If the potassium level falls low enough, life-threatening disturbances of heart rhythm can result. Enlargement of the parotid and salivary glands can occur because of binge eating and vomiting. Recurrent vomiting can result in erosion of tooth enamel, gastroesophageal reflux disease, and inflammation or tears of the esophagus. Some individuals consume so much food during a binge that their stomach or esophagus ruptures. Fortunately, such events are very rare because they are usually fatal.

MEDICAL COMPLICATIONS OF BINGE-EATING DISORDER

As we have already noted, most individuals with binge-eating disorder are overweight or obese and therefore are at risk for developing the medical problems associated with being overweight, such as diabetes and high blood pressure. However, there is no good evidence that individuals with binge-eating disorder are at higher risk for these complications than are individuals of similar weight who do not have binge-eating disorder.

MEDICAL COMPLICATIONS OF ARFID

Research on ARFID is still in its early stages, so detailed information about its associated medical complications is not available. However, if the eating disturbance leads to weight loss, individuals with ARFID are at risk for the medical problems associated with anorexia nervosa, as described earlier. On the other hand, if the eating problem is characterized by the consumption only of a few high-fat foods, like French fries, the individual may be at risk for weight gain, nutrient deficiencies, and even obesity.

Future Prospects

Throughout this chapter, the often grim litany of what is and is not known about eating disorders—and of all that can go wrong as a result once they have developed—belies one critically important point: that most people with these disorders do in fact recover from them, especially if the disorder is recognized and appropriately treated early.

> Most people with these disorders do in fact recover from them.

Among adolescents, up to 70% of those with anorexia nervosa recover over time, and 20% improve but continue to have residual symptoms, while the remainder chronically struggle with the disorder. Relapse, or a return to disordered eating behavior after initially successful treatment, is a common occurrence, and the illness does have one of the highest mortality rates among psychiatric disorders. The mortality rate during adolescence is low, however, and ultimately, the most positive outcomes are seen in individuals between the ages of 12 and 18 with a short duration of illness.

The majority of adolescents and adults with bulimia nervosa also improve over time, with recovery rates ranging from 35% to 75% after 5 or more years. The illness is rarely fatal, and again, early diagnosis and treatment are important factors in recovery. Recovery from binge-eating disorder is also very common as this disorder is quite responsive to a wide range of treatments.

The road ahead for you as the parent of an adolescent with an eating disorder will not be easy. You may face months, perhaps even years, of helping your child with all the challenges the illness presents. But together, and with the right interventions from qualified professionals, you can take this battle on and win it.

Valerie says of her daughter Audra, now an adult whose struggle with anorexia nervosa began 15 years ago, "She received good treatment, poor treatment, and no treatment. She has been treated as an outpatient and an inpatient. She has been incorrectly diagnosed, received drugs she did not need, and lost in between the cracks of systems that were not trained to recognize eating disorders. Because of her anorexia, she has had heart irregularities, osteoporosis, and has lost some kidney function. Since her release from the hospital, life has included a round of trips to numerous doctors and will continue that way until her psychiatrist thinks she has been in remission long enough to spread the doctor visits further apart.

"Still, after all that, our daughter has achieved a fairly normal life. She has gotten married, has a daughter, attends family functions, goes to church, and would like to have another child in a few years. She sometimes talks about the possibility of returning to school and becoming a physical therapist. She struggles daily with her weight and her willingness to eat. She knows that this is something that will be with her for the rest of her life but getting the right treatment has helped her to want to keep on going. The dreams are alive."

> "Getting the right treatment has helped her to want to keep on going. The dreams are alive."

Michael's mother Diane adds: "If your child is recovering from anorexia nervosa, the most important thing a parent can do is to make sure they maintain the 'goal' weight range set by the doctor and understand that if your child is still growing the 'goal' may be a moving target for a little while. Reaching [that weight range] was tough for Michael, but the closer he got to it, the better his brain functioned, and he eventually started to understand that going back to a low weight at any time would be dangerous because it could start the cycle all over again. We will hold on to that for a long time so that he can keep thinking clearly and stay focused on his recovery."

Chapter Three

Getting the Right Treatment for Your Child

Therapy, Medication, and More

Facing the possibility that your child may have an eating disorder is only the first step toward getting him or her help. The next step is to find the right kind of help, a task that can feel overwhelming at first. Where do you start? Since eating disorders involve both psychological issues as well as physical complications, should you initially approach a general practitioner or consult a psychologist? Or should you find someone who specializes in eating disorders? If the diagnosis of an eating disorder is confirmed, what will the treatment for it involve, and how long will it take? Does your child need to be hospitalized? How much will treatment cost, and will your insurance cover it?

All of these are important considerations when taking the initial step toward finding treatment for an adolescent with an eating disorder. To help you make informed choices as you and your child go through the treatment process, this chapter surveys the various settings (e.g., hospitalization, outpatient), approaches (e.g., psychotherapy and medication), and relapse prevention methods that you may encounter along the way. Guidance on how to navigate the healthcare system is offered as well. We will offer ideas about how to approach the conversation about treatment with your teen in the following chapter (p. 123).

Finding Treatment: Where to Begin

All eating disorder experts recommend that the first step is to make an appointment with a general practitioner, typically a pediatrician or a specialist in adolescent medicine, and ideally someone your child knows and trusts, such as your regular pediatrician. A medical assessment will be necessary to determine your teen's general physical condition as well as to rule out other causes for symptoms like rapid weight loss or gain, low pulse rate, or low energy. It is also crucial in determining whether immediate intensive intervention, such as hospitalization to address medical instability due to anorexia nervosa or bulimia nervosa, is needed. Necessary as this assessment is, however, it is sometimes inconclusive: routine physical tests, such as blood work, are often entirely normal and may be of limited use in establishing the diagnosis. Therefore, because it is so critical to recognize and treat these diseases early, ask the physician for a referral to someone who specializes in eating disorders, just to be sure. As Audra's mother Valerie says, "It has been my experience that some members of the medical community are less knowledgeable than others in the recognition or treatment of eating disorders. With anorexia or bulimia nervosa especially, by the time they recognize a problem, the patient can already be in a life-threatening situation. With binge-eating disorder, clinicians might think to ask about changes in mood and anxiety and even eating patterns, but not to ask specifically about eating that feels out of control. If your insurance company won't cover the consultation, find a specialist and make the appointment yourself, and then be prepared to pay for it yourself."

> Ask the physician for a referral to someone who special-izes in eating disorders.

The prospect of finding a qualified specialist on your own can seem daunting, but there are numerous organizations—such as local mental health associations and professional psychiat-ric or psychological organizations—that can offer assistance and referrals for providers in your area. Another option is to contact your health insurance carrier for a referral, which will also ensure that treatment will be covered under your policy. Additionally, there are many national eating disorders associa-tions that can aid in finding treatment. Their names, phone numbers, and addresses are listed in the Resources section at the end of this book (p. 211).

If the doctor does positively confirm that your child has an eating disorder and gives you a referral to a specialist, don't make the call with the expectation that your child will be able to see the specialist the next day. Because of the limited num-ber of professionals specializing in eating disorders, some treat-ment providers have substantial waiting lists for their services, and you may have to wait weeks, perhaps even months, before one of them can see your child. The delay, combined with the worry about what is wrong with your child, can increase ten-sions within your family, as Donna explains.

"Because Chelsey was exhibiting signs that made us suspect she had an eating disorder, my husband Eric and I insisted she see the family physician who'd been treating her since she was a little girl. She fought it, but we wouldn't budge, so she eventually went. Once there, the doctor recommended having an evaluation at a specialized center for eating disorders. Eric and I were relieved because we thought she'd get the help she needed right away, but it took 2 whole months for her to even be seen by someone there. During the waiting period, we had to physically monitor her, which really put a strain on our relationship with her. She just couldn't understand that we were doing it to help her. Anyway, once she was finally evaluated, the specialist at the center recommended residential treatment, which Chelsey adamantly refused, so I agreed to drive her there every day as an outpatient on the condition that if she lost even 1 ounce, she'd have to be admitted. It wasn't an ideal situation for any of us, but at least she was finally getting some help."

> "She just couldn't understand that we were doing it to help her."

What Does Treatment Involve?

As is the case for almost all serious illnesses, the treatment of eating disorders is both an art and a science. Science provides the facts—about what treatments are known to work, what treatments are known to be ineffective, and what the complications are of different treatments. The scientific basis for the treatment of eating disorders, especially among adolescents, offers a lot of promise but it is, of course, far from complete. The art lies in combining the incomplete scientific base with a sense of what is a good "fit" for a particular adolescent who lives in a particular family in a particular community, and in constructing a treatment approach that will be acceptable and effective. The practitioner's experience and his or her ability to work well with the adolescent and the family are crucial elements of the art of treatment.

Since the 1990s, a growing consensus has developed among health professionals and among the organizations that pay for treatment, like insurance companies and the government, that all medical treatment should be "evidence-based." That is, the only treatments that should be used (and paid for) are the ones that have proved to be effective through rigorous scientific studies. In theory, this is an excellent principle. However, in many areas of medicine, including eating disorders, the evidence base is smaller than anyone would like, often making it challenging for providers to confidently make evidence-based recommendations. On the other hand, since the first edition of this book almost 15 years ago, a significant amount of new research has been conducted so that treatment recommendations for adolescents with eating disorders, including those treatments we will describe in this chapter, can be based both on this new knowledge and on extending to adolescents the knowledge about adults.

There is a broad consensus that therapy should begin as soon as possible after the diagnosis has been established, with the treatment provider(s), parents, and patient working together to individualize treatment. Unfortunately, as Donna's story illustrated, the setting for treatment as well as the optimal provider is likely to be determined, at least partially, by availability.

A comprehensive plan to address all of the complexities of the disease should incorporate medical, physical, and nutritional monitoring; psychotherapy; and, in some instances, medication. A variety of different professionals, including physicians (psychiatrists, primary care providers, pediatricians, or adolescent medicine specialists), psychologists, social workers, and nutritionists familiar with syndromes like anorexia nervosa, bulimia nervosa, binge-eating disorder, and ARFID can play key roles in the effectiveness of treatment. Therefore, it may take time to find the treatment plan and providers that best suit your child as well as the rest of your family. In addition, it is important for you to be aware of the treatment options and to use your own judgment about what is right for your child and your family.

Effective treatment is built, at least in part, on an establishment of trust between your child and the treatment team. This trust doesn't happen overnight, and most of the parents interviewed for this book stressed the long time it took to find a provider or providers who had a good fit with their child. Among the challenges to overcome will be the fairly heady resistance that your child will likely exhibit to treatment in the first place. For example, people with bulimia nervosa or binge-eating disorder may believe that the treatment recommendations will make them gain, or not lose, weight. Those with anorexia nervosa may initially assume that the only goal of treatment is to make them gain weight. And those with ARFID may believe that treatment will ask them to eat in "dangerous" ways, in which they might feel nauseous or choke. In any of these cases, the affected individual may be reluctant to confide in treatment providers or to stay in treatment for more than a short time. After one or two sessions, for example, your daughter might tell you she no longer needs to see a therapist or that she can stop the disordered-eating behavior on her own. But, in fact, even with good treatment, it can take a long time for someone to recover from an eating disorder.

Effective treatment is also built on a good working relationship between parents and the treatment team, especially in family-based approaches. For teens with anorexia nervosa especially, there are data to support that parents are an integral part of the treatment equation. As a parent, you can play an important part in sustaining the resolve—both your child's and your own—to give the treatment process and your child's providers enough time to work and to show positive results. At the same time, however, you should remain vigilant: if after a reasonable period you see that your child isn't progressing (e.g., is still losing weight or continuing to show signs of binge eating, purging, or significantly limiting types of food eaten), it may be necessary to search for other approaches and providers.

Professional Guidelines for Assessing and Treating Eating Disorders

Several professional organizations have developed guidelines to help practitioners assess and treat adolescent eating disorders. In 1999, the United Kingdom established a National Institute for Clinical Excellence (NICE) which conducts extensive literature reviews and publishes guidelines on the treatment of a wide range of illnesses, including eating disorders. The most recent revision of the NICE guidelines for eating disorders was published in 2017 and is almost 1,000 pages long. The NICE guidelines make detailed recommendations for the identification, treatment, and management of eating disorders in children, adolescents, and adults and has substantial information for parents. The NICE guidelines recommend family-based therapy (a specific type of family psychotherapy described later in this chapter) as an essential tool in treating eating disorders during adolescence and notes the importance of monitoring growth and development and, for individuals with anorexia nervosa, assessing bone health.

The Society for Adolescent Health and Medicine (SAHM) includes professionals in medicine, nursing, psychology, public health, social work, nutrition, education, and law. The SAHM provides guidelines for the treatment of eating disorders that were updated in 2015. Among the key recommendations are that family-based therapy should be viewed as a first-line psychological treatment, that most adolescents can be treated as outpatients, and that weight restoration and resumption of menses in girls are important treatment goals for those with anorexia nervosa.

The American Psychiatric Association also provides guidelines for psychiatrists. These were first published in 2006 and updated in 2012; a new revision is currently under way. The recommendations are quite similar to those of NICE and the SAHM.

All of these guidelines recommend family-based therapy, but such treatment can seem intimidating at first. As Audra's mother Valerie says, "We love our daughter very much and had spent a long time attending individual, family, and group therapy. We were willing to do anything that might help her. For years, we had listened to one mental health professional after another tell us that Audra's problems were our fault, so we always thought we had to shoulder that enormous burden of guilt. When our daughter began seeing a therapist who specialized in treating eating disorders, the best thing for us as parents was that we were finally told we had not caused her illness. You can't imagine how relieved we were to find out we were not to blame."

Therefore, if the treatment team recommends family-based therapy sessions, don't be reluctant to attend because you fear you will constantly be under attack or accused of causing your child's problems. As discussed in Chapter 2, the fundamental causes of eating disorders are unknown. A good therapist will not get into the "who's to blame" game but will instead focus on your child's recovery and on your participation as a vital component in that process. Diane's experience with the treatment her son Michael received illustrates this point.

> A good therapist will avoid getting into the "who's to blame" game.

"When Michael was admitted to the eating disorders clinic, the doctor and others there said that it didn't matter why he got sick. All that mattered at that point was that his health was restored. Sometimes you never quite know why a child gets sick, and it can hold you back if you focus too much on that aspect of treatment. The first priority is that your son gets well, which also takes the pressure off of him because he isn't constantly being bombarded with the 'why's.' Looking forward instead of looking back can make all the difference in the recovery process."

Once you have identified a potential treatment provider, it will be helpful to ask him or her some questions, such as the following:

- What is the diagnosis of my child's eating problem?
- How many teenagers with this sort of problem have you treated?

- Have you identified any other important emotional or psychological problems, like depression or substance use? (See Chapter 2, pp. 46–50.)
- What treatment setting is most appropriate (inpatient, outpatient, or an intermediate level of care)?
- What type of psychological counseling do you recommend?
- Do you recommend the use of any medications?
- How often will you see my child?
- To what degree will our family be involved in treatment, and how often will information about my child's progress be shared with me?
- How is my child's physical condition going to be monitored (including who will weigh my child and how often)?

For most of these questions, there are no absolutely "correct" answers. Rather, they provide a basis for beginning an important dialogue with the person who will be helping to care for your child. It is very important that you and the treatment provider understand each other's perspective and that you are comfortable with the provider's plan to treat the eating disorder. If the treatment provider is not especially experienced with treating eating disorders, but access to a specialist is limited in your geographic area, you might ask about whether the provider will seek consultation with specialists elsewhere if necessary. The National Eating Disorders Association (NEDA) has posted on its website material on "how to help a loved one" as well as a Parent Toolkit which includes similar questions that you can also ask treatment providers. (For more information, see the Resources section at the end of the book.)

It is very important that you and the treatment provider understand each other's perspective.

Once you've found a specialist or treatment program that suits your child's needs, the sequence of specific interventions will be determined, in part, by the need to address the more acute and medically serious problems first. Several important goals to achieve, in order of decreasing urgency, include

- Correct potentially life-threatening health complications (e.g., heart irregularities, low blood pressure, dehydration)
- Minimize risks of self-harm, such as suicidal behavior
- Restore weight to normal
- Eliminate binge eating and purging
- Develop normal eating behavior
- Address psychological and psychosocial issues (e.g., low self-esteem, body image distortion, problems in interpersonal relationships)
- Maintain long-term recovery

Where Will Treatment Take Place?

Where and how your child will be treated will depend largely on the severity of the physical and psychological symptoms of the eating disorder and any related problems. Broadly speaking, the prevailing wisdom is that, whenever possible, youth with eating disorders benefit from remaining "in their lives"— that is, living at home, attending school, remaining involved with friends and extracurricular activities. Certain aspects of typical teen life, such as excursions with friends, may even ultimately be leveraged as rewards for engagement in treatment. For this reason, outpatient treatment that involves the family (and especially the parents) is, in many instances, the first-line intervention for adolescents with eating disorders. However, this is just one of many treatment settings and, depending on circumstances, may not be where the specialized treatment journey begins. If, for example, your daughter's or son's health is compromised to the point of potentially life-threatening medical complications, she or he would first need to be physically stabilized before other interventions can be considered. Close medical monitoring on an inpatient basis is warranted especially for individuals whose anorexia nervosa has reached an acute stage. Appropriately trained healthcare professionals can usually treat bulimia nervosa on an outpatient basis, but some individuals with this disorder need to be monitored for potential medical complications as well. Frequent medical monitoring may also be required for those with ARFID who are significantly underweight or experiencing nutritional deficiencies as a result of highly restrictive eating behavior. The various options are further explained next.

Medical Hospitalization

In the most severe cases of eating disorders, short-term hospitalization in a medical unit (sometimes in an intensive care unit) is required to stabilize and then monitor your child medically. Vital signs (blood pressure, heart rate and rhythm) will be watched closely, and the acute physical effects of malnutrition and of binge eating and purging will be treated with fluids and medications. If the patient is underweight, refeeding will be initiated orally or, if necessary, by means of intravenous or nasogastric feedings. Hospitalization usually lasts anywhere from 3 to 10 days, depending on how severe the medical problems are and how the patient responds to rehabilitative efforts.

Inpatient Psychiatric Treatment

Inpatient psychiatric care differs from short-term medical hospitalization in that, once a patient is medically stabilized, treatment efforts can focus more intensively on behavioral and psychological issues. Most inpatient psychiatric units are located in a general hospital and often provide care not only for patients with eating disorders but also for patients with other psychiatric problems. A few medical centers in the United States have inpatient units devoted primarily or exclusively to the care of individuals with eating disorders. Such inpatient units may be best equipped to deal with the most severely ill and most complicated patients. Meals are closely supervised, and intensive individual and/or group psychological treatment is provided. Conditions that may coexist with the eating disorder (e.g., depression, an anxiety disorder, or obsessive-compulsive disorder) are carefully assessed and appropriate treatments initiated. Most eating disorder inpatient units have 24-hour clinical support available from physicians, psychiatrists, psychologists, nurses, and nutritionists. The average length of stay is 1 to 4 weeks, depending on the patient's response to treatment and on how much insurance and other financial support is available (see the section "Navigating the Healthcare System" in this chapter). For some families, inpatient treatment works; for others, it doesn't. It is perhaps best conceptualized as a chapter of care that can ready a patient for continued outpatient treatment, either by jump-starting renourishment and weight restoration or by breaking a cycle of binge eating and purging.

"We had been in counseling for a year when Linda relapsed," Kay says of the initial treatment they were pursuing for her daughter who struggled with bulimia nervosa. "During that relapse, the counselor realized Linda needed something more. She discussed sending her to a psychiatrist about 50 miles away, but then I found a large university that had a general psychiatric unit with some patients with eating disorders. Even though it was over 80 miles away, I thought it looked like a better option because it had a whole treatment team."

Linda was hospitalized twice for a total of 9 weeks. "It was inpatient," Kay says. "But as I found out after the first hospitalization, they merely stabilized her medically. They did provide therapy, nutritional counseling, and helped us find a therapist in our area. However, they really didn't give Linda the tools she needed to help her deal with situations after she got home. I would never do a hospital-type setting again. I think a small residential setting would be better. It would be more personalized. The big university hospital had too many doctors involved, and you received too much conflicting information. Things were always changing, and we weren't informed. They also had no informational classes for parents, and we felt totally excluded from her treatment."

Conversely, Diane has nothing but praise for the treatment her son Michael received for anorexia nervosa in a large, university-affiliated eating disorders unit. "The care he got was exceptional, and the doctors always kept me informed of what was going on with his treatment. Because it was an academic medical center, I felt reassured that he was getting care based on the most up-to-date research. Being one of two boys on the unit also worked out fine for him. Some guys might have hated it, but because all the women there wanted to get better, it was a very positive and encouraging environment for Michael. Everyone was very supportive and nurtured him and built him up. As much as he hated being in the hospital,

I know their support—in addition to that of the doctors—really helped him."

Residential Care

Residential care can be described as inpatient treatment on a smaller scale and in a less medical and more "home-like" environment than in large hospitals. The average stay in a residential care program is usually about a month. Most (but not all) commercial insurance plans include coverage for care in a residential treatment setting, but an exception to this might be federal and state public insurance policies (e.g., Medicare, Medicaid).

The first residential center devoted to the treatment of eating disorders opened in 1985. In 2006, there were 22 such programs, and there are now more than 75. Most of these are "for profit" businesses, and much of this expansion has been supported by venture capitalists. Residential centers advertise heavily on the Web to both professionals and patients. Many of these programs offer sound, evidence-based interventions, such as weight restoration for underweight patients and cognitive-behavioral therapy (CBT), but some offer interventions that have little empirical support. To date, clinical outcome information from residential treatment programs is limited. While many programs provide some data on their websites as part of promotional marketing efforts, this information has not typically been through a rigorous review process as would be the case for publication in an academic journal. Interest in peer-reviewed clinical outcome data from residential treatment programs is growing, and, in the years to come, we hope that more information will be available to families considering treatment in this setting.

In considering admission to a residential center, there are a number of specific questions you should ask to assess the potential appropriateness and effectiveness of the program:

- Would a trial of outpatient care be appropriate first?
- What is the level of training and experience of the therapists providing the treatment? (Do they have PhD, master's, or bachelor's degrees? From whom did they learn the treatment technique? For how many years have they been treating individuals with eating disorders?)
- What specific evidence-based treatments (such as CBT and family-based treatment) are provided, how (individual vs. group sessions), and how often?
- For individuals admitted with anorexia nervosa, what is the average rate of weight gain? (The best *inpatient* programs help underweight patients gain 3–4 pounds per week; residential programs generally cannot do as well, but less than 2 pounds per week—or not knowing the average rate of weight gain!—would be worrisome.)
- What fraction of individuals admitted with anorexia nervosa are discharged at a minimally acceptable weight, so that their body mass index (BMI) is at least 18.5?

> "As much as he hated being in the hospital, I know their support . . . really helped him."

Both inpatient treatment and residential care may be crucial for adolescents whose physical states are at the critical stage, but the prospect of watching your child being "locked up," as one mother put it, can certainly be very upsetting.

"There is nothing you want more than for your child to be home with you," says Valerie, whose daughter Audra was treated for anorexia nervosa. "But as I found out the hard way, you can't 'police' them 24 hours a day, nor do you have the skills to deal with all of the complex aspects of the disease that's overwhelmed them. And I have to admit that, once my daughter was finally admitted to a long-term residential care facility, I felt a tremendous sense of relief about not being in the position of constantly having to try to 'save' her. I could just be a parent again. I was able to visit her on a weekly basis, which gave me the opportunity to be supportive and encouraging instead of being the nasty witch who forced her to eat or tried to stop her from doing 300 sit-ups in the middle of the night."

Partial Hospitalization Program or Day Hospital Care

Often recommended for those making a transition from an inpatient or residential facility, a partial hospitalization program (PHP) is a daily program, usually lasting 4–8 hours, that provides structured eating situations and active treatment interventions while allowing the individual to live at home and participate in certain school activities. Such programs may also be recommended as the first intervention for adolescents who need close supervision but not the 24-hour care provided in hospital and residential settings.

Intensive Outpatient Therapy

Intensive outpatient therapy (IOP) requires patients to come to an outpatient clinic for several hours on several days per week. IOP and PHP programs differ by the number of hours or programming they include but are otherwise similar. IOPs are group-based programs that include supervised eating, commonly used to help individuals transition from the more intensive PHP level of care to something less structured, en route to discharge from a specialized program to outpatient treatment in the community. Insurance plans may cover PHP and not IOP or vice versa, so programs may offer both in order to accommodate more individuals.

Outpatient Care

As noted earlier, except for life-threatening situations, outpatient therapy is the most widely used form of treatment for adolescents with eating disorders. Sessions are often scheduled once a week but may occur more frequently for patients who need more intensive help or less frequently for patients who are improving and can maintain more normal eating habits with less clinician contact. The teen is able to live at home and attend school but consults regularly with members of his or her treatment team (e.g., physician, psychotherapist, dietitian or nutritionist). Family-based therapy sessions are an integral part of outpatient treatment for teens, involving parents, other caretakers (e.g., grandparents, nannies) and, if appropriate, siblings.

What Is the Best Treatment Setting for My Child?

One of the toughest decisions for a parent is about where treatment should occur: inpatient, residential, outpatient, or somewhere in between. A number of factors must be weighed in making this decision, but here are a few generally accepted principles. There is broad agreement that it's best to choose the least restrictive environment that provides effective treatment but allows the adolescent to continue with his or her normal school and social life; accordingly, an outpatient setting is often recommended for mildly to moderately severe eating disorders. On the other hand, severe medical complications, such as extremely low weight or dangerous laboratory abnormalities, almost always need to be treated in an inpatient setting where close medical monitoring is provided. Residential or intensive outpatient treatment may be appropriate when an adolescent is medically stable but is struggling to control frequent behavioral disturbances like binge eating or vomiting. Because of the disruption to normal life entailed by residential treatment, clinicians often want to give treatment on an outpatient basis a try before utilizing a higher level of care. And, as we have emphasized throughout this book, if, after several weeks, a particular treatment or treatment setting is not producing significant change, such as an increase in weight for individuals with anorexia nervosa or a decrease in binge eating for those with bulimia nervosa or binge-eating disorder, it is important to consider making a change.

> One of the toughest decisions for a parent is about where treatment should occur.

Psychological Treatments

Psychotherapy, or psychological counseling, is an integral component of treatment for eating disorders. Research studies of adults, especially of those with bulimia nervosa and binge-eating disorder, have shown that such psychological approaches are clearly useful. The most promising treatment outcomes in psychotherapy studies of individuals with anorexia nervosa are those of children and adolescents with a recent onset of the disorder. A number of research studies in the past 15 years have clearly documented the benefits of family-based treatment for anorexia nervosa, and a smaller number of studies suggest that this approach is likewise useful for bulimia nervosa. Although research on the treatment of ARFID is at an early stage, there is good reason to believe that a family-based approach is useful. As we noted earlier, the treatment guidelines from professional organizations endorse this approach. Based on solid knowledge regarding the treatment of adults with eating disorders and more limited information from studies of adolescents, there is good reason to believe that other forms of psychological treatment, such as CBT, are also useful.

If your daughter or son has been diagnosed with anorexia nervosa, bulimia nervosa, or binge-eating disorder, the type of treatment she or he receives will depend not only on her or his needs but also on the availability of knowledgeable practitioners and their experience with different treatment approaches. In the next section, we briefly describe what to expect from each of these therapies. Then we summarize the amount of information available about which of these approaches may be most effective for particular types of eating disorders. Though the psychotherapies described differ somewhat in theory and practice, they have several features in common. First, these talk therapies are focused on the here-and-now, concerned with the current symptom cycle of the eating disorder, rather than the exploration about why the eating problem developed. Second, these therapies are directive, with therapists taking an active role, listening, teaching skills, and strategizing ways through barriers to progress. Third, these therapies tend to be fairly structured (and even the least structured of the options is likely to be supported by the structure of a treatment team doing regular monitoring of symptoms, weight, and medical status). Most essentially, the psychotherapies that help eating disorders symptoms the most aim to effect change in eating behaviors. If eating behavior changes (and for those who are underweight, if weight gradually normalizes), then the therapy is helping; if not, this is a good reason to consider a change in treatment approach.

Family-Based Therapy

As the name suggests, family-based therapy involves bringing members of the patient's family together for group sessions to identify and change the patterns that may contribute to and/or arise from a teen's eating disorder and to open lines of communication and teach everyone coping skills for dealing with the illness. Other goals may include strengthening family bonds, reducing conflict in the home, and improving empathy among family members.

The specific form of family-based therapy that has been most widely studied and that is recommended by most treatment guidelines was initially developed at the Maudsley Hospital in London and is sometimes referred to as the "Maudsley method." (Several excellent books have been written about this method, including James Lock and Daniel Le Grange's *Help Your Teenager Beat an Eating Disorder* [2015].) This form of family-based therapy was specifically designed for adolescent patients with anorexia nervosa; it has also been used for those with atypical anorexia nervosa and is quite unlike other, more generic family-based programs. Instead of focusing on the psychological roots of disordered eating, this family-based therapy is aimed specifically at addressing problematic eating behavior and emphasizes the participation of the family as a vital component to the success of treatment. For teens with anorexia nervosa, there are three phases of treatment.

The first phase focuses on weight restoration and attempts to change behavior by initially transferring control of the patient's eating to the parents. In other words, you as the parent will be empowered to and responsible for "refeeding" your child. While the term *refeeding* might conjure up images of having to tie your daughter down and force-feed her, in this case it simply means using food as medicine you administer to help your child get well, just as you would give her antibiotics if she had a severe infection. All meals are prepared and supervised by parents as they help renourish their child.

During this phase, food and eating behavior are also explored as part of the family dynamic. For example, you might be asked to bring a picnic to a therapy session. While you and your family arrange place settings, dole out food, and then eat, the therapist (who does not partake of the meal) asks questions about who plans the meals at home, who buys the groceries, who prepares the food, who serves the food, and so on. Once the picnic is over, the therapist can then offer observations about ways in which your family communicated, socialized, formed allegiances, and dealt with other issues revolving around food behavior during the meal. These insights can help you to understand the effects that the disease has on your child as well as on the rest of your family, and to learn how all of you can work together to help her reach the goal weight set by her doctor.

> Food and eating behavior are also explored as part of the family dynamic.

Once your child's weight has been restored, the second phase of this method begins. During this phase, responsibility for maintaining weight is gradually transferred to your child. Parents are helped to determine the age-appropriate and child-specific correct degree of control and autonomy for their child. For example, an adolescent might resume eating lunch unsupervised at school, making her own after-school snack, or going to dinner with friends 1 or 2 nights per week. In the final phase, treatment begins to focus more on general family and individual concerns, with the therapist providing problem-solving skills for both your daughter and your family to help prevent the recurrence of anorexia nervosa. The emphasis is on returning to a healthy, balanced life, which, for a family with an adolescent, includes the typical developmental struggles that may have been ignored due to the eating disorder.

Given the merits of family-based therapy for adolescents with anorexia nervosa, the treatment was subsequently adapted and tested for use with bulimia nervosa. The primary distinction between family-based therapy for adolescent bulimia nervosa versus anorexia nervosa is that, in the former, the adolescent is encouraged to collaborate with parents in their effort to facilitate recovery. This more collaborative approach is possible because adolescents with bulimia nervosa are more likely to experience their symptoms as distressing. Another difference is the focus on disrupting the cycle of binge eating and the subsequent compensatory behaviors, rather than weight restoration.

Similar to family-based therapy for anorexia nervosa, treatment is divided into separate phases. First, parents are empowered to re-establish healthy eating in their adolescent and to supervise post-meal time to prevent the use of compensatory behaviors. After the eating pattern is normalized, control of eating is gradually returned to the adolescent, under the parents' supervision, just as it is in family-based therapy for anorexia nervosa. The final phase of treatment begins when the adolescent can eat normally without parental supervision and focuses on general individual and family concerns.

Individual Psychotherapy

Individual psychotherapy ("talk therapy") is a private, one-on-one intervention that occurs between a trained therapist (such as a psychiatrist, psychologist, or social worker) and a patient, usually once or twice a week. Several different theoretical approaches underlie and direct what the therapist does and says in individual psychotherapy. We will describe the major theoretical perspectives, but we should emphasize that, while they may seem quite different from each other on paper, in practice, many therapists combine elements from them all.

COGNITIVE-BEHAVIORAL THERAPY
CBT was developed for adults with depression in the 1960s and is based on the theory that persistent but maladaptive thinking patterns are key contributors to emotional disturbances. A substantial body of scientific evidence supports the effectiveness of CBT for the treatment of depression and anxiety disorders, both in adults and in adolescents. Beginning in the 1980s, CBT was tailored specifically to the treatment of eating disorders.

> Beginning in the 1980s, CBT was tailored specifically to the treatment of eating disorders.

As the name implies, CBT focuses on "cognition" (e.g., one's views and perceptions of oneself) and "behavior" (e.g., one's actions in response to those perceptions), with the aim of correcting those ingrained patterns of thought and behavior that may be contributing to one's illness. The cognitive part of CBT helps people to identify unrealistic thoughts or habitually pessimistic attitudes and to reframe them in more realistic or optimistic terms. The behavioral part of CBT helps people to change the way they react to the world around them by developing better coping strategies for dealing with their interpersonal relationships and their illness.

As applied to eating disorders, the primary importance of CBT lies in its exploration of the individual's idealized body weight and shape and of his or her behavioral reactions to that idealization. For example, if your daughter fears gaining weight, she might start to restrict her food intake in rigid and unrealistic ways, such as by fasting. However, the fast then leaves her completely starved, both physiologically and psychologically, which in turn leads to a voracious need to satisfy her hunger through binge eating. The episode of binge eating is then followed by purging (e.g., vomiting, laxative abuse, or diuretic abuse) as she attempts to reduce shame and anxiety about possibly gaining weight from the binge. Additionally, binge eating and purging can cause distress and low self-esteem, thereby fostering conditions that lead to more dietary restraint followed once again by binge eating.

To interrupt this vicious cycle, CBT applies cognitive and behavioral procedures designed to modify the individual's unrealistic attitudes about shape and weight and to help her both resume regular eating patterns that include the consumption of previously avoided foods and develop constructive skills for coping with high-risk situations that might trigger binge eating and purging. These same procedures can also help to prevent the individual from relapsing back into her bulimic behaviors at the conclusion of treatment.

EXPOSURE THERAPY

Exposure therapy—formally known as exposure therapy and response prevention (or ERP)—is a specific form of CBT in which patients work during and between sessions to confront feared stimuli without using ritualized "safety" behaviors. It is considered a first-line intervention for children, adolescents, and adults with OCD, social anxiety disorder, and specific phobias. The purpose of ERP is to provide people with a chance, in session, to see that what they fear is unlikely to happen and that, even if it does, they will be able to manage it. Repeated practice during and between sessions typically helps individuals to become accustomed to feeling anxious, sometimes to habituate to it, and always to act in the service of health and flexibility rather than always to avoid what they fear.

This approach distinguishes itself from the others described in this chapter because it is experiential in nature. After creating a hierarchy of eating disorder–related fears—things like types of food, eating situations (e.g., choosing from a buffet, ordering quickly off of a menu, eating dry food without drinking water), clothing (e.g., tank tops, fitted pants, bathing suits), and beyond—the therapist and patient work together in every session to tolerate fears without engaging in corresponding rituals (such as selecting only "safe" foods like salad from a buffet, readjusting items of clothing). ERP sessions may involve doing unusual things to stay in contact with anxiety or other difficult feelings. For example, if an adolescent with ARFID has a fear of choking on food, he may be asked to put a lot of dry crackers in his mouth and let them sit there or to eat a few tablespoons of peanut butter without taking any sips of water. If an adolescent with anorexia nervosa has a fear that eating salad with dressing on it will make her gain weight, she may be asked to eat it during session while cinching a belt around her waist to mimic the feeling of fullness and fatness. Mirror exposure for a normal-weight, weight-stable adolescent may involve wearing increasingly "challenging" outfits, looking in the mirror, and describing oneself in neutral, factually descriptive language. Because they are experiential in nature, ERP sessions may be longer than typical individual psychotherapy sessions.

INTERPERSONAL PSYCHOTHERAPY

Interpersonal psychotherapy, often referred to as IPT, has its origins in psychodynamic psychotherapy but differs in several important respects. IPT was developed in the 1980s as a short-term (12–16 sessions) treatment for depression among adults and focuses primarily on the individual's social functioning. The therapist is quite active in helping the patient identify problem areas, such as "role transitions," and uses several specific techniques, including role playing, to help the patient develop new methods of dealing with his or her interpersonal relationships.

In research studies of depressed adults, IPT has been found to be very helpful, so much so that it has been adapted specifically for adolescents struggling with depression (renamed IPT-A) and, again, has been clearly demonstrated to be effective. IPT-A focuses on several difficulties of obvious importance to adolescents, including separation from parents, relationships with members of the opposite sex, and peer pressures. It would appear to have much to offer in the treatment of adolescents with eating disorders as its methods are well described, it addresses interpersonal issues that many adolescents with eating disorders struggle with, and it is effective for depression, a condition that commonly affects teens with these syndromes. Indeed, within the realm of eating disorders, IPT is recognized as a viable alternative to CBT for adults with bulimia nervosa and binge-eating disorder. It has been successfully adapted (in group format) for use with teens who experience loss of control eating and are at risk for obesity, but it has not otherwise been studied in adolescents.

In contrast to CBT, IPT does not directly focus on eating behaviors or body shape and weight concerns. Rather, the theory underlying IPT is that disturbances in eating behavior including binge eating and/or purging occur as a response to interpersonal stressors and negative mood. Therefore, the emphasis in treatment sessions is on identifying and addressing the interpersonal problems that maintain or worsen mood and eating disorder symptoms and teaching and practicing communication skills that may help improve functioning in relationships.

DIALECTICAL BEHAVIORAL THERAPY

Dialectical behavior therapy (DBT), originally developed to treat chronically suicidal adults meeting criteria for borderline personality disorder, is, broadly speaking, a well-studied psychotherapy for adults and is used to treat teens with mood disorders who experience intense emotional shifts, suicidal thoughts and urges, and self-harm. It is a "third-wave behavior therapy" that evolved from CBT. It has been less rigorously tested in adolescents with eating disorders but may be good for teens who experience frequent suicidality, engage in self-harm behaviors, or explicitly use behaviors like purging as a means to self-harm. Whereas a CBT approach tends to help people develop strategies that prevent a particular emotion response from being activated, DBT helps people to modulate the expression or experience of an emotion after it has begun. In addition to teaching adaptive coping strategies, skills to enhance interpersonal effectiveness are introduced and practiced, including skills related to mindfulness, acceptance, and metacognition (i.e., thinking about one's thinking).

The basic premise of DBT for eating disorders is that disordered eating serves to regulate otherwise intolerable feelings in individuals with too few adaptive strategies for managing their emotions. Binge eating and purging behaviors are theorized to result from trying to escape or block unpleasant emotions that may be triggered by thoughts regarding food, body image, or other aspects of the self and to provide relief from these feeling states. DBT can be delivered in an individual format, with or without a complementary skills group. A skills group teaches traditional strategies for each of three DBT domains: mindfulness, emotion regulation, and distress tolerance. In the treatment of people with eating disorders, sometimes a fourth domain—"eatingness"—is also covered. This involves exploration of the ways in which our current cultural and nutritional environment can be invalidating of true physical and emotional health, as well as psychoeducation about weight regulation and the effects of starvation.

PSYCHODYNAMICALLY-ORIENTED, SUPPORTIVE PSYCHOTHERAPY
Although no reliable statistics are available, it is likely that this traditional form of individual therapy continues to be commonly employed for adolescents with any kind of psychological problem, including an eating disorder. This approach has its historical roots in the psychoanalytic traditions of Sigmund Freud and his disciples, and it exists in many varieties. Their common thread is a focus on the patient's inner, unconscious (i.e., below the surface) psychological experience, based on the assumption that the patient's unresolved psychological conflicts and uncertainties produce emotional upheaval and lead to behavioral disturbances, including those central to eating disorders.

One of the most appealing aspects of this form of individual psychotherapy for a person with an eating disorder is its one-on-one format, which provides a safe environment where feelings can be shared without worrying about who might approve or disapprove of what is being said. Adolescents with eating disorders may be reluctant to express themselves honestly at home, at school, or in social circles for fear others will disapprove of what they might say. Low self-esteem can cause them to remain silent because they think their opinions don't warrant attention. For a teen with anorexia nervosa who feels inadequate or unable to discuss her problems, refusing to eat is a powerful option for expressing herself without having to say a single word. For a teen with binge-eating disorder, eating in response to emotion is a short-term salve that may leave him ashamed or embarrassed and even more unlikely to express difficult thoughts and feelings. But in sessions with a therapist who is supposed to be an objective, nonjudgmental observer a reticent teen has the opportunity to talk openly about troubling relationships at home, social pressures at school, and other factors that can contribute to the development and maintenance of the eating disorder. Additionally, understanding and confronting the roots of feelings such as inadequacy or worthlessness can enable her to eventually find other ways of coping with life's problems besides waging a fierce battle against the natural needs of her body.

> Refusing to eat is a powerful option for expressing herself without having to say a single word.

The effectiveness of individual psychotherapy, especially one using the psychodynamic approach, depends on the bond formed between the patient and the therapist, and it normally takes a while before they actually "click." It's important to reemphasize this point, especially if your daughter or son comes to you after only one session and tells you she or he hates the therapist and doesn't want to go back anymore. This may be a natural response. Try to talk your child through this resistance by telling her or him as gently as possible that getting to know someone doesn't happen right away, perhaps even providing an outside example. As one mother put it, "It took my daughter a few months to understand that her therapist wasn't the enemy, the anorexia was. Once she finally got it, she actually started looking forward to her therapy sessions and would come home chattering about anything that popped into her head. It was quite an amazing difference from the silent, sullen girl who had previously referred to her therapist as 'that big jerk.'"

> "It took my daughter a few months to understand that her therapist wasn't the enemy, the anorexia was."

Even if the fit between patient and therapist is excellent, you should be aware of a worry some experts have about the psychodynamic approach to eating disorders. There is no scientific proof that anorexia nervosa, bulimia nervosa, binge-eating disorder, or ARFID is, in fact, caused by "underlying" psychological problems or that resolving underlying issues inevitably leads to the resolution of the eating disorder. It is certainly important for any therapy to address problems with self-esteem and to help the youngster understand what he or she is going through. But it is also important that the symptoms of the eating disorder, including weight loss, binge eating, and purging, be frequently monitored and addressed in some way. Therefore, it may be good if someone in addition to the psychodynamic therapist, like the pediatrician or the nutritionist, keeps an eye on these symptoms.

In other words, as noted previously, if your child doesn't seem to be progressing after a certain period of time with this treatment (indeed, with *any* form of treatment), you have the option of finding someone else with whom she or he might feel more comfortable or who takes a different approach. Several parents interviewed for this book emphasized just this point. "My advice to other parents is to always remember you have choices," Susan said. "I wasn't pleased with the way Vanessa's therapy was going, but didn't say anything because I thought, 'Well, she's in the hands of a professional. They must know better than I do about what she needs.' As it turned out, the therapy wasn't a good fit at all, my daughter completely relapsed, and I kept kicking myself for not following my instincts. If your kid isn't getting better, it's imperative to keep trying to find someone else until she does."

Group Therapy

Another therapeutic option is group therapy. In this method, group sessions are usually led by a mental healthcare professional (e.g., psychiatrist, psychologist, social worker), who facilitates a dialogue among patients trying to recover from similar problems. In the case of eating disorders, a group therapy session might consist of discussions about body image, the importance of food (both psychologically and physically), social problems, or other issues that the group leader might think need addressing. Group therapy sessions are commonly used in more intensive treatment settings, like hospitals and day programs, and may involve preparing and eating meals, receiving nutrition education from a dietician/nutritionist, or learning skills specific to a psychotherapy such as CBT, IPT, or DBT.

Since many people with eating disorders tend to isolate themselves and avoid speaking out about their problems or feelings, group therapy may not work for everybody. Still, as part of a comprehensive treatment program, it can help some adolescents to share their feelings with others who understand what they're going through. The outcome seems to depend on who is leading the sessions and the individuals involved, but little research has been conducted to validate the ultimate effectiveness of this therapy.

What's the Right Psychological Treatment for Your Child?

Among the various psychological approaches used to treat eating disorders, which one will work best for your child's particular type of eating problem? Unfortunately, it is not possible to know in advance exactly which form of treatment will be just right for a specific person. Some people quickly understand the CBT approach and learn to use it very effectively, while, for others, it just doesn't seem to click. In the following sections, we describe what research tells us about the overall effectiveness of different forms of treatment for different disorders. We suggest that you try to locate a clinician experienced in providing the type of treatment that research currently suggests is the most effective and get your child into treatment with him or her as soon as you can. Then, after the first month or two of treatment, make a clear-eyed assessment of how your child is doing. For example, if the problem is anorexia nervosa, has your child gained weight? If the problem is bulimia nervosa, has the binge eating and purging stopped or has their frequency dropped significantly? If the problem is ARFID, is your child beginning to eat a wider repertoire of foods? Multiple studies have shown that the best predictor of how effective a treatment will be in the long run is how quickly it starts to work. Therefore, after a reasonable length of time—a month or two—if your child's symptoms are not clearly improving, it may be time to consider a different form of treatment.

> It is not possible to know in advance exactly which form of treatment will be just right for a specific person.

FOR ANOREXIA NERVOSA

Only a few studies have scientifically compared the utility of different forms of psychotherapy for adolescents with anorexia nervosa, and these have focused primarily on the family-based therapy described earlier that was developed at the Maudsley Hospital. The good news is that these studies are uniformly encouraging about the effectiveness of this approach. Most of the adolescents treated did very well, with a majority returning to a normal or near-normal weight while in treatment and sustaining their recovery after treatment ended. As reflected in the current treatment guidelines from professional organizations, the results of these studies have led most experts to recommend this approach as the first intervention to try for adolescents with anorexia nervosa.

Two recent findings suggest potentially useful variations on the standard family-based treatment for anorexia nervosa. One recent study compared family-based treatment to the same treatment approach but delivered only to the parents—the adolescent did not attend the sessions with the therapist. The results were impressively positive, with the "parent-focused treatment" doing at least as well or better than the usual family-based treatment. Second, a number of centers specializing in the treatment of eating disorders have invited multiple families to attend treatment sessions together (sometimes referred to as a "multifamily group") and found that families successfully learn from one another. You may want to discuss these options with your treatment providers.

A continuing unanswered question about the family-based approach is how well it compares to other methods of treatment, especially individual psychotherapy. The studies that are available either have not examined that question or are too few for us to be fully confident of the results. For example, CBT is clearly helpful for adolescents with other problems such as depression, is the treatment of choice for adults with bulimia nervosa, and appears to be useful for adults with anorexia nervosa. So there is good reason to think that CBT would be helpful for adolescents with anorexia nervosa. But until the results of more studies are available, the family-based treatment method should be considered the leading treatment for adolescents with anorexia nervosa.

For Bulimia Nervosa

Although not as extensively studied as for anorexia nervosa, family-based treatment has been examined in the treatment of adolescents with bulimia nervosa and appears quite useful. For adults with bulimia nervosa, CBT is widely considered the treatment of choice, and there is reasonable evidence that it is also useful for adolescents. Furthermore, it has been used successfully to treat teens for conditions that often coexist with an eating disorder. It has, for example, resulted in faster remission of adolescent depression than that produced by alternative forms of psychotherapy, including family and supportive therapy. There is also good evidence of the effectiveness of CBT in children with anxiety disorders, both at the end of treatment and for a number of years afterward. If similarly applied to the treatment of bulimia nervosa in teens, the procedures that comprise CBT are likely to produce similarly positive results.

> CBT in treating adolescents with bulimia nervosa is unproved, but it has been used successfully to treat teens for conditions that can coexist with an eating disorder.

IPT, while not quite as effective as CBT for adults with bulimia nervosa, is nonetheless useful. And again, it has been successfully used to treat teens with depression, which in turn suggests it as a potentially promising approach to the treatment of adolescent bulimia nervosa.

FOR BINGE-EATING DISORDER

As yet, there has been little research on how best to treat binge-eating disorder and loss of control eating among adolescents. One recent study suggests that IPT is useful, particularly for adolescents who also experience high levels of anxiety. Since CBT is of proven benefit to adolescents with mood and anxiety disorders, which often co-occur with binge-eating disorder, it is also a sensible option.

FOR ARFID

Research on ARFID, including how best to treat it, is only just beginning. Preliminary reports suggest that it is important to involve parents and to focus directly on the eating behavior. Some investigators are adapting CBT to specifically address issues that frequently arise in individuals with ARFID, including the use of ERP within a course of CBT. In many cases, it is helpful to have the involvement of a multidisciplinary team including, for example, a pediatrician, psychologist or psychiatrist, and nutritionist.

FOR OTHER ADOLESCENT EATING DISORDERS

As discussed in Chapter 2, a considerable number of adolescents have an eating disorder that does not meet the criteria for an eating disorder formally defined in *DSM-5* and therefore have what is considered an OSFED. Very little research has examined how best to treat individuals with a specific OSFED such as purging disorder or atypical anorexia nervosa. Therefore, if your child has a disorder that falls into the OSFED category, the best approach in thinking about what treatment would be best is probably to choose the treatment(s) of proven benefit for the officially defined eating disorder that most closely resembles your child's problem. For example, it would be reasonable to consider family-based treatment or CBT for an adolescent with purging disorder or with atypical anorexia nervosa.

Medication

As a parent, it's likely you'll need to deal with the issue of medication while your child is in treatment for an eating disorder. The most common type of "psychotropic" (mind- or mood-altering) medications prescribed for individuals with eating disorders are antidepressants, such as those listed in Table 3.1.

> It's likely you'll need to deal with the issue of medication while your child is in treatment for an eating disorder.

A modest number of studies of antidepressants have been conducted in anorexia nervosa. Several of them were done decades ago and evaluated antidepressants that are now only rarely used. Several more recent studies have tested antidepressants in the newer and safer class, namely, the selective serotonin reuptake inhibitors (SSRIs) such as fluoxetine (Prozac). But, consistently, nothing more than a slight therapeutic effect, at most, has been found. Because antidepressants have proved

Table 3.1 Commonly Prescribed Antidepressants

Type of antidepressant	Generic name	Usual brand name
Selective serotonin reuptake	citalopram	Celexa
inhibitors (SSRIs)	escitalopram	Lexapro
	fluoxetine	Prozac
	fluvoxamine	Luvox
	paroxetine	Paxil
	sertraline	Zoloft
Other "modern" antidepressants	bupropion	Wellbutrin
	desvenlafaxine	Pristiq
	duloxetine	Cymbalta
	mirtazapine	Remeron
	venlafaxine	Effexor

quite useful in treating other conditions that can accompany anorexia nervosa (e.g., major depression disorder or anxiety disorder), the fact that these drugs provided at most a slight effect is both surprising and disappointing. Some researchers believe that the malnutrition inherent in anorexia nervosa depletes serotonin and might interfere with the therapeutic action of antidepressants, especially SSRIs. In other words, the lower the patient's weight the less effective the drugs will be. Diane's son Michael was started on the SSRI paroxetine (Paxil) before he entered an eating disorders clinic, and it had little effect.

"In the long run," she says, "the drug didn't do much for him because his weight was so low when they started him on it. His doctor informed me that because his brain had suffered from the effects of starvation and malnutrition, just like all the other parts of his body, drugs like Paxil wouldn't be effective until he started gaining weight. Still, he stayed on it until he reached his goal weight and then came off it soon after that. His doctor had no strong feelings about the medication and left it up to Michael to decide. Michael really wanted to be off it, and we all agreed he could stop. He had no problems coming off it and everything worked out fine. I'm not sure if the Paxil made a difference, but his attitude changed completely as he began to regain weight."

> "The drug didn't do much for him because his weight was so low."

Apart from antidepressants, *atypical antipsychotic drugs*, a class of medication usually used to treat mental disorders like schizophrenia or bipolar disorder (manic depression), have also been considered as a possible treatment for acute anorexia nervosa because of their association with weight gain. Recent research has now established that olanzapine (Zyprexa) provides a modest benefit in helping adults with weight gain. Unfortunately, it has little effect on the psychological symptoms of anorexia nervosa, like the obsession with shape and weight, and it can have side effects, so most clinicians recommend it only if the initial psychological and behavioral treatment approaches are not sufficiently effective. Given the anxiety that occurs in anticipation of and during mealtime for people with anorexia nervosa, anti-anxiety medications like alprazolam (Xanax) also have some theoretical appeal. Unfortunately, they don't appear to be dramatically helpful in alleviating anxiety (or improving eating behavior) and, in general, are not widely employed. In addition, they have some potential for abuse and addiction.

For bulimia nervosa, virtually every class of antidepressant medication has been studied in trials for adult patients with this disorder, and the evidence is quite clear that antidepressants help patients control their binge eating and purging. It is not clear that any particular medication is the most effective, but, in general, SSRIs are generally well tolerated, so they are usually the first-choice pharmacological treatment for adults with bulimia nervosa. Specifically, the SSRI fluoxetine (Prozac) is the only drug approved by the US Food and Drug Administration (FDA) for the treatment of bulimia nervosa in adults. Results of a small trial reported in 2003 suggest that this drug is well tolerated by and may be useful for adolescents with this illness as well.

In the research studies, antidepressant treatment for bulimia nervosa reduced rates of binge eating and vomiting by sometimes up to 75%, with both depressed and nondepressed patients with bulimia nervosa responding equally well to these drugs. It should be noted, however, that many patients with eating disorders are reluctant to use medication and a significant number end treatment prematurely. Moreover, despite convincing evidence of the effectiveness of this class of medication for the treatment of bulimia nervosa, residual symptoms of the illness persist in many of those treated.

A range of different medications, including a number of antidepressants, have been examined in research studies of adults with binge-eating disorder. Virtually all produce significant drops in the frequency of binge eating and improvement in mood, but most have no impact on weight, a fact that is often disappointing, as most patients with binge-eating disorder are overweight and wish to lose weight. Recently, the stimulant medication lisdexamfetamine (Vyvanse) was tested in several large studies of adults and found to lead to a significant decrease in binge frequency and a modest loss of weight.

On the basis of these studies, in 2015, the FDA approved the use of lisdexamfetamine for the treatment of adults with binge-eating disorder. No studies have examined the utility of medication for the treatment of binge-eating disorder among adolescents, but lisdexamfetamine has been approved for and is widely used to treat attention deficit hyperactivity disorder (ADHD) in children and adolescents. Therefore, it might be considered for an adolescent with a significant problem with binge eating. On the other hand, lisdexamfetamine can have side effects, and it is likely that its impact on eating behavior and on weight will last only as long as the medication is being taken.

As always when medicines are used, the patient's response must be monitored so that adjustments can be made if necessary. Shirley's daughter Jody, who was struggling with bulimia nervosa, did not have a good response to medication, but it is possible she might have if she had been more closely observed.

"Jody became depressed and anxious as a result of her binge/ purge behaviors, so drugs were prescribed," she says. "She took Paxil for depression, as well to reduce the urge to purge. She was also given Ativan for anxiety. Unfortunately, their effectiveness was limited because a physician didn't monitor the dosages. A psychiatrist had prescribed the meds on the recommendation of Jody's psychologist, but there was never any follow-up. In many cases, the prescribed dosage of a drug can make all the difference in how the person responds to it. But because of negative side effects, Jody eventually made the decision to take herself off the drugs. I'll never know what might have happened had the dosages changed or she'd been prescribed different medications."

Safety must be a primary consideration when prescribing psychotropic medications for adolescents with eating disorders, especially for those who are medically unstable and therefore may be more vulnerable to experiencing side effects. Also of concern were reports that appeared in the early 2000s that SSRIs may increase the risk of suicide in young people. These concerns led the FDA in 2004 to issue a Public Health Advisory about the increased risk of suicidal thoughts and behavior ("suicidality") in children, adolescents, and young adults being treated with SSRIs and other antidepressant medications. More recent reviews of relevant studies indicate that the link between antidepressants and increased suicidal ideation and behavior in youth is quite weak, and there is a broad consensus among mental health professionals that, for conditions for which antidepressants are helpful, the benefits clearly outweigh the risks. It is worth noting that the eating disorders themselves are associated with an increased risk of suicide and therefore that effective treatment of the eating disorder will also reduce that risk.

Clearly, the decision to put your own child on medication should be based on a careful consideration of his or her circumstances and state of mind, and it is essential that you play an active role in the decision-making process by discussing with your child's doctor the pros and cons of the medication that might be prescribed. In the course of your discussion, you might ask such questions as

> It is essential that you play an active role in the decision-making process.

- What are the generic and brand names of the medication?
- What is it supposed to do?
- How soon should we see results?
- When and how often should my teen take the medication?

- How long should my teen stay on the medication?
- Will my teen need to limit any activities while taking the drug?
- Does the medication interact with alcohol, other drugs, or certain foods?
- What are the possible side effects of the medication?
- Which of these side effects are most serious?
- Will there be challenges of coming off of this medication?

Carefully monitoring your child's behavior after a medication has been started is also imperative, not only to ensure that he or she is taking the drug as prescribed but also to watch for improvements in symptoms or for certain red flags that may indicate an adverse reaction to its effects. If your child is prescribed an antidepressant, for example, you should immediately notify the doctor if the following symptoms develop or become worse: anxiety, panic attacks, agitation, irritability, hostility, impulsiveness, extreme restlessness, insomnia, self-injurious behavior, and suicidal thoughts.

Nutritional Counseling

Nutritional counseling is sometimes a piece of the multidimensional approach used in eating disorders treatment. It is typically provided by registered dietitians with specialty training in this area. The dietitian's role and responsibilities vary depending on the treatment setting. Of note, nutritional counseling is typically *not* a part of family-based treatment because, in that modality, parents are empowered to help their child in whatever ways are consistent with treatment goals, including renourishment and weight restoration, within the family milieu.

Across settings, nutritional counseling can include experiential exercises, including practice with portion-sizing, grocery shopping, food preparation and cooking, or dining out in public (commonly referred to as "meal support"). It is commonly used in conjunction with talk therapy to support weight maintenance and normal eating patterns in individuals stepping down from care in structured treatment like an inpatient or residential program to an outpatient setting. It may also be a useful addition to talk therapy if your child has a diet-related medical condition, such as type 1 diabetes, celiac disease, or food allergies, or a co-occurring psychiatric disorder which may need to be prioritized in their psychological treatment. For overweight teens with binge-eating disorder, nutritional counseling is utilized primarily to reduce binge eating rather than to target weight loss, unless that is medically indicated (in which case it would follow normalization of the eating pattern). Finally, nutritional counseling can be quite helpful during the transition from adolescence to young adulthood as the responsibilities associated with living independently for the first time during or after college (such as grocery shopping, food preparation and cooking) can be quite daunting for a young person with an eating disorder.

Other Useful Strategies

In this day and age, we'd be remiss to write about advances in eating disorders treatment without at least briefly reviewing e-mental health resources and how they are being applied to eating disorders treatment and overall psychological well-being. Simply put, technology is ubiquitous, and the electronic delivery of interventions to people as they go about daily routines is increasing exponentially. By-and-large, scientifically based conclusions about the merits of these interventions lag behind the technological advances. However, electronic interventions potentially harness incredible power in improving access to the basic principles of eating disorders treatment, extending the benefits of psychotherapy beyond the therapy session, and supporting prevention of relapse (a risk we will come to next).

Currently, several different apps (i.e., smartphone applications) are available that may be relevant for individuals with eating disorders, though the landscape is shifting so rapidly that the examples provided here today will likely be outdated tomorrow. How parents choose to monitor their child's use of technology, in general, is of course under the purview of each particular family. When it comes to eating- and weight-related apps on the market, parents should be aware that the vast majority encourage restrictive eating and weight loss and that these are contraindicated for adolescents with eating disorders whose goals may include renourishment, flexibility with food choices, cessation of calorie-counting or excessive exercise, and adherence to a regular schedule of meals and snacks.

The most common function of apps developed specifically with individuals with eating disorder in mind, such as Recovery Record and Rise Up + Recover, is a simple focus on monitoring of eating behavior and meal planning. Rather than encourage fine-grained attention to food content, monitoring on these apps allows for individuals to fill in a text box loosely describing what and how much they ate or to take a photograph of their meal. These apps can be set with reminders to eat at regular intervals and can be personalized to query for the presence or absence of eating-disordered behaviors at or after mealtime. Teens, digital natives who do not remember a time before text message was possible, tend to find electronic methods of self-monitoring to be less burdensome than pen and paper, and the personalization/reminders built in to the functionality of these apps can be especially helpful in keeping them on task with treatment goals. If your child's clinician is recommending the use of an app in treatment, familiarize yourself with the program's features and discuss with your teen and her or his therapist any specifics about the use of the app that concern you. Recovery Record and Rise Up + Recover both allow for ease of connection with treatment providers, either by the patient syncing data directly with their clinician or by being able to export and send summaries of records to a clinician. The preliminary qualitative reports on user experience of Recovery Record suggests that some adult patients find connection to the clinician through the app to be a supportive treatment enhancement, while others viewed it as an interfering deterrent.

Aside from apps specifically developed for people with eating disorders, apps aimed to deliver elements of psychotherapies deemed especially helpful for the treatment of these conditions may prove beneficial. A number of CBT-based apps guide users in monitoring and challenging problematic beliefs; coping with anxiety, sadness, and stress; working through steps of problem-solving; and supporting overarching behavior change. DBT-informed apps include reminders of distress tolerance and emotion regulation skills, which may be especially helpful to someone experiencing a moment of emotional difficulty *in that moment*. There are also several popular apps aimed at the general population that offer guided meditation and breathing exercises with the goal of stress reduction and relaxation.

Relapse Prevention

Relapse is defined as the reappearance of eating-disorder symptoms or the deterioration of a person's condition following an initially successful response to treatment. For example, if your son was treated for anorexia nervosa and his weight was restored, you should suspect a relapse if he starts losing weight again, begins exercising excessively, or avoids family meals. For bulimia nervosa, indications that your daughter might be relapsing following treatment could include self-disparaging remarks about how fat she's gotten or signs that she's binge eating and purging again. Decreased dietary variety and/or flexibility with eating may signify the start of a relapse into ARFID.

Relapses are indeed common among people with eating disorders, but just how common is unclear. Figures on the actual rates of relapse are imprecise, largely because the research on this subject is not consistent in its use of key terminology to characterize the continuum of experiences—the ups and downs—that may occur between a person's initial treatment and that person's ultimate recovery. Terms like *treatment response, relapse, remission,* and *recovery* tend to be used differently from one scientific study to the next, which makes relapse estimates from different studies difficult to compare. This variation also undermines attempts to establish standardized guidelines for effective relapse prevention, defined as maintenance therapy for individuals who have completed initial treatment and achieved a certain measure of symptomatic recovery. To further complicate matters, no matter the definition used, relapses can and should be distinguished "lapses." Lapses can include an infrequent experience of feeling out of control while eating, undereating at an occasional meal, or getting on a scale every day. Lapses are expected, and, in fact, toward the end of treatment, therapists typically help patients consider how they will respond to a lapse to prevent a full relapse.

> Relapses are indeed common among people with eating disorders.

With all that said, the following surveys what, on balance, are estimated to be the relapse rates for anorexia nervosa and bulimia nervosa and describes what is currently known about the types of relapse prevention that have been tried with patients who have these illnesses.

Relapse Rates and Relapse Prevention for Anorexia Nervosa

The majority of patients with anorexia nervosa who are hospitalized due to the severity of their illness respond well to treatment as inpatients. Unfortunately, follow-up studies indicate that the post-hospital period is fraught with difficulty, showing a significant resurgence of symptoms and relapse rates generally ranging between 30% and 50%, with some rates as high as 70%. Moreover, the rates are as significant for adolescents who require hospitalization as they are for adults. In a study of 95 patients between the ages of 12 and almost 18 years old, for example, nearly 30% of those who successfully completed their inpatient program relapsed following discharge.

Despite these sobering figures, the findings of at least one study (of post-hospitalized adults) do indicate a positive prospect: that if the weight restoration achieved during hospitalization is maintained for a year after discharge, the risk of subsequent weight loss declines dramatically. In other words, the longer a patient can maintain a normal weight after hospitalization, the lower the risk of relapse, so the first few months following discharge are crucial.

The same types of psychological treatments that we described previously are also used to prevent relapses in the post-hospital period for anorexia nervosa. The family-based method of treatment for anorexia nervosa was, in fact, originally designed as a post-hospital treatment, delivered over the course of 1 year following inpatient care. The findings from the initial study of this method reported that it was more effective than individual supportive therapy for individuals whose age of onset for anorexia nervosa was 18 years or younger and whose illness had a duration of less than 3 years. Treatment gains in this group were largely maintained at a 5-year follow-up assessment, suggesting that changes initiated by family-based therapy serve to prevent relapses and to enhance the treatment's long-term effectiveness for patients with anorexia nervosa.

What about the use of medication in relapse prevention? As noted earlier in this chapter, antidepressants are not effective in treating anorexia nervosa in severely underweight patients, nor are they effective in reducing relapse once weight has been restored. Whether olanzapine, which is of some short-term benefit, might have a role in the prevention of relapse has not been tested.

Relapse Rates and Relapse Prevention for Bulimia Nervosa

Relapse rates for adult patients with bulimia nervosa are estimated at around 30%. No clinical trials evaluating psychological treatments for acute symptoms of bulimia nervosa have specifically focused on relapse prevention for this disorder; instead, relapse prevention is typically an integrated component of the initial treatment. Most studies suggest that the majority of adults who respond well to initial CBT, the best evidence-based treatment for bulimia nervosa, continue to do well after these interventions have ended, with the most enduring recovery occurring in those people who achieved full remission of binge eating and purging by the end of treatment. Similarly, in the few studies of adolescents with bulimia nervosa, the gains made during treatment with family-based treatment and with CBT appear to be reasonably well maintained over the succeeding year. There is strong evidence that antidepressant medications are useful in the treatment of adult patients with bulimia nervosa, at least in the short term, but how long medication treatment should continue in order to sustain improvement is unclear. Most psychiatrists believe that the rate of relapse is greater when medication is discontinued after only a few months and recommend that medications be continued for at least 6 months.

At least one of the parents interviewed for this book expressed a wish that when her daughter relapsed with bulimia nervosa, she had been prescribed an antidepressant. "When Linda was hospitalized the first time, the doctors didn't think she was depressed," Kay says. "She was the cheerleader of the ward. That was because she had such a good way of hiding her problems. Her friends didn't even know she was bulimic. One time while she was in the hospital, she asked one of the doctors if she could go on antidepressants, and he told her she could if she were hospitalized again. Then, when she was hospitalized again, I asked another doctor on the ward about medication, and she replied that she felt cognitive-behavioral therapy was better. Well, we had been doing that for over a year and here we were again. I wish we'd had the chance to try medication. I know it isn't always the answer and many times the kids won't stay on it, but it would have been nice to think we tried."

"She was the cheerleader of the ward. That was because she had such a good way of hiding her problems."

Relapse Rates and Relapse Prevention for Binge-Eating Disorder

There is good evidence that most individuals who respond to psychological treatment such as CBT or IPT for binge-eating disorder are able to sustain that benefit for months to years thereafter. There are few studies of the long-term outcome of individuals with binge-eating disorder treated with medication. However, a recent study found that discontinuation of lisdexamfetamine after 3 months of successful treatment was followed by a relapse in about one-third of adult patients. In routine practice, most clinicians suggest continuing medication for at least 6 months if it is helpful.

What to Do If Your Child Relapses

The bottom line for you as the parent of an adolescent with an eating disorder is vigilance and then preemptive action at the first signs of a relapse. If you have even a slight suspicion that your child is slipping back into disordered eating patterns after an initially successful course of treatment, it is important that you contact his or her treatment provider(s) as relapses can often be more severe than the first occurrence of the disease. As Donna recalls, one summer Chelsey "fell into a deep depression and the anorexia returned. She denied it, of course, but I finally told her she had to go back to the eating disorder clinic. The doctor there was very worried about her health, did an abbreviated assessment, and said she was in critical condition, that she was even sicker than she'd been when she was there the first time. That's why I think it's important for other parents to know what they're in for, which might involve years of dealing with a seemingly successful recovery followed by relapse."

Relapses can often be more severe than the first occurrence of the disease.

Ultimately, as Donna's experience suggests, you may need to hold steady in your resolve to support your child's recovery over the long haul and to work closely with his or her providers throughout the twists and turns that the recovery process may take. These illnesses are complex, and, even in adults, on whom most of the research has been conducted, they can be frustratingly stubborn to resolve. The same is true for adolescents. But with vigilance and persistence, you'll go a long way toward helping your child overcome the various challenges the eating disorder and its treatment may present.

Navigating the Healthcare System

It is a sad fact that the battle against these extremely difficult illnesses is sometimes made more difficult by the healthcare system itself.

"When Chelsey went to the doctor," Donna says, "I was told she was in critical condition and needed to be admitted immediately for inpatient treatment. I called our health insurance company to make sure treatment would be covered.

When they said no, my husband and I decided we had to admit Chelsey regardless and could fight about the insurance later. I then got a call from the hospital's business office telling me that Chelsey's care would cost $1,600 a day. I again called the insurance company, and, after a lot of contentiousness, they finally agreed to pay, but only for 3 days. The doctor told us the treatment would take much longer, but that without it, Chelsey would die. So my husband told the people at the hospital we'd pay for whatever the insurance didn't cover. After Chelsey was admitted, I was relieved about the fact that she was finally getting treatment. However, the better I felt about her, the angrier I got about our insurance company refusing to pay. I set out on a campaign to make them pay. It eventually worked somewhat because they finally agreed to pay for 7 days of inpatient treatment, but that was it. They refused to pay for more. With Chelsey in treatment for over a month, you can figure out just how much the insurance didn't cover.

"The worst part of it all, besides the exhaustive fighting back and forth almost daily, was that Chelsey thought she was destroying our family because she was so worried about how much her care was costing. What a crime it is to put a person who is sick in that position."

> "Chelsey thought she was destroying our family because she was so worried about how much her care was costing."

Because eating disorders often require a broad range of treatment for both physical complications and psychological issues, many health insurance providers balk at footing the bill. If a company does cover eating disorders, it usually has very specific guidelines that limit treatment substantially. Consequently, like Donna, many parents of adolescents with eating disorders find themselves not only helping their child battle a potentially life-threatening disease but also waging war against insurance carriers who nickel-and-dime them about every little bit of treatment their child so desperately needs.

When President Bill Clinton signed the Mental Health Parity Act of 1996, it was viewed as the first step in eliminating discrimination against individuals with mental illness. Taking effect on January 1, 1998, the landmark law mandated that employers who have more than 50 workers and who offer group health insurance must not place any limits to coverage for mental illness that are any greater than limits placed on coverage for medical or surgical conditions. As the Centers for Medicare and Medicaid Services (CMS) states, "If your health plan has a $1 million lifetime limit on medical and surgical benefits, it cannot put a $100,000 lifetime limit on mental health benefits."

But there's a catch: although the law mandates "parity" for the treatment of mental illness with regard to dollar limits, it does not require group health plans to offer mental health coverage if their benefits packages don't already do so. Only those group plans that already provide mental health benefits and are sponsored by employers with 50 or more workers are subject to the law.

Mental health parity legislation has undergone several revisions with improvements on both the state and federal levels since the initial version more than 20 years ago, including the Mental Health Parity and Addiction Equity Act of 2008 and then the Patient Protection and Affordable Care Act of 2010 (also called the "Affordable Care Act"). Nevertheless, there are often hard-to-navigate guidelines used by insurance companies to determine "medical necessity," a criterion that governs their willingness to reimburse for care, with different companies using different criteria and sometimes being poorly informed about the seriousness of eating disorders. Additionally, existing state parity laws were not preempted by the federal law, so depending on what state you live in, certain coverage remains in effect, which can, on occasion, exclude certain conditions like eating disorders.

What does all this mean to you as a parent, and how can you make sure your insurance carrier pays for the treatment your child needs to recover from an eating disorder? On its website, NEDA has material on insurance and related legal issues, including how to fight for appropriate and necessary care (https://www.nationaleatingdisorders.org/learn/general-information/insurance). Highlights include

- Get a complete assessment that includes a medical evaluation of your child so as to develop a whole picture of what type of care is needed (e.g., inpatient, partial hospitalization, residential, outpatient).
- As soon as a certain treatment plan has been advised, ask your insurance company or healthcare provider for recommendations to programs or specialists covered under your plan. Request a copy of your full insurance policy from the insurance company. Understand whether you have out-of-network benefits, and, if so, what these benefits cover as well as the out-of-network deductible for your policy.
- Should the company representative you speak with tell you your child's needs are not covered under your plan, ask to speak with the medical director of the company. Ask the medical director about a single-case agreement, which is determined on a case-by-case basis and allows an individual to use in-network benefits to

seek out-of-network care. Insurance companies provide single-case agreements when in-network providers do not have the clinical expertise to provide necessary treatment or in-network providers are not able to begin specialized treatment in a timely manner.

- Every time you speak to someone at the insurance company, make sure to write down that person's name as well as the date and time of the conversation. If you put any requests for services in writing, make copies of everything before mailing. Such documentation may be necessary for you to prove your efforts to secure payment (e.g., in case your insurance company tells you that they have no record of your phone calls or that your written requests were never received).

- If all of your attempts fail to secure some type of payment from your insurance company, pay for it yourself (as Donna did) and then continue to pursue reimbursement.

- Notify your state insurance commissioner if you have been denied insurance coverage.

Some of the parents whose experiences inform this book lost their children to the consequences of an eating disorder. In Donna's case, that loss was compounded by her insurance company's adamant refusal to provide adequate coverage for the treatment Chelsey needed. "Unlike some people in this country, I've never been 'sue happy,'" says Donna. "But I wanted to send a message to the company that denied my daughter a chance to recover from the deadly disorder that had overwhelmed her. When we were paying our hard-earned money for premiums every month, the company was only too happy to take it. But when it came time for them to pay back, they insisted our coverage was too limited and wouldn't accommodate certain treatments Chelsey desperately needed. That's why I decided to pursue a lawsuit against them." In fact, in some states, legal action by parents has led to substantial changes in how much coverage must be provided by insurance companies.

Valerie's daughter Audra has survived anorexia nervosa, but their experience with insurance providers was no less frustrating. Valerie offers the following advice:

"The best thing I can tell other parents about fighting the system is to write letters or send emails to all of your government officials. The longer your child is denied treatment, the greater the chance that the disease will be fatal. It's true that government officials always pass on the requests to someone else, but it's been my experience that most requests eventually do wind up on the desk of someone who will take action. The more letters you send, the better, and don't bother to wait for responses. Just keep sending pleas for assistance as fast as you can get them out." Patients and families can contact their state's attorney general's office if they believe the coverage offered by the insurance company is inconsistent with parity legislation or fair coverage of a medical or psychiatric condition. Many attorneys general are pursuing parity legislation cases or helping to push insurance companies to do right by their beneficiaries, helping the companies decide to resolve the coverage issue in order to avoid legal action.

"If your child is on Medicaid," Valerie adds, "don't give up. You'll inevitably be told that treatment is not covered or that the state doesn't have the money to pay for treatment. I was even told one time that 'anorexia is a weight gain/weight loss disorder and we don't cover that.' If I had been asking for help for a heart condition, kidney failure, or osteoporosis—all of which were symptoms my daughter displayed at the time—she could have received immediate treatment. However, since her primary diagnosis was anorexia, the insurance company did not want to pay for treatment. So you must continue to make calls and write letters until your child is accepted in a treatment program. If everybody keeps at it, maybe one day all those government officials who received letters from grieving parents begging for help will change the laws so that mental illnesses and physical illnesses are treated the same under insurance."

Kay reiterates Valerie's advice:

"Keep pushing your insurance carriers. You will get frustrated, but don't give up on trying to find the right care for your child and don't give up on your child. You never know what combination of treatments will work. It's never the same for any one person and that's why eating disorders are so difficult to treat."

"You will get frustrated, but don't give up."

Chapter Four

Daily Life with the Teen Who Has an Eating Disorder

Helping an adolescent face and then overcome an eating disorder raises some unique challenges for parents, and indeed, for the outer circle of other adults—a teacher or an athletic coach, say—who may play an active role in that teenager's life. This is true both before and after the individual has received treatment for the illness. If your daughter is showing signs of bulimia nervosa, you might be wondering how best to confront her about this possibility. Or you might be worried that your son, who was treated for anorexia nervosa, may be slipping back into patterns you thought were safely in the past, such as obsessing about food and calories, exercising feverishly, or wearing oversized clothes. Or you might be a coach or a teacher who has noticed that your star runner on the school track team is forcing herself to throw up before every race or that your straight-A math student seems listless and is excruciatingly thin. You might be a guidance counselor who is concerned when you notice a student who has become socially withdrawn and has noticeably gained weight, wondering if he is depressed, or binge eating, or both. Or you might be a close family friend who notices that your friend's child is scared to eat dinner at your house whenever you host a sleepover.

Adults confronted with the possibility that their child or a child they know might have an eating disorder face many dilemmas: What is the best approach to take when talking to the teen, and how should you prepare yourself for the conversation? If your child has already been treated for an eating disorder, what can you do to assure progress toward recovery? Also, what support is available for *you* as you try to help a child not only face her disorder or cope with his illness, but also survive and get beyond it? Can teachers, coaches, or other adults in a teen's life assist in this effort and in effect serve as a second line of defense, behind the first line that parents and healthcare professionals represent, in the fight against these syndromes?

This chapter offers some basic tips for parents and other adults on navigating the difficult waters of everyday life with a child who has an eating disorder, whether that disorder is only suspected or is now confirmed. These recommendations summarize information given in some of the resources listed at the end of this book, but they also draw on the personal experiences of parents themselves and on the practical wisdom they've gleaned from facing these disorders in their own children. Varied as their experiences are, they all speak to a single reality: that you can and do have a very important role to play in helping a teenager beat an eating disorder, whether you're the parent of that teen or another adult with a direct connection to that child's daily life.

> You can and do have a very important role to play in helping a teenager beat an eating disorder.

The advice in this chapter is by no means intended as a substitute for professional treatment. This is especially true in the event of a medical emergency. If a teenager you know is showing major indications of having an eating disorder (e.g., extreme weight changes, dizziness or blackouts, profound depression) or is a suicide risk, it is imperative that you not take time to debate with that child about the need to get help. You must take action and get professional attention for the child immediately. As we emphasized in Chapter 2, the medical consequences of eating disorders or of their possible concurrent conditions are severe and potentially fatal, and the sooner an adolescent begins treatment, the better his or her chances are of recovery. The tips in this chapter may help you to avert an emergency in the first place or to handle the aftermath of a crisis if one in fact does occur, but they are not stand-ins for medical advice or treatment. Those can come only from a qualified professional who knows the details of the teenager's problem.

Getting the Teen to Treatment: Communication and Persistence

Talking to adolescents can be difficult under the best of circumstances. Due to physical and psychological changes, academic stress, and peer pressure, formerly outgoing kids can grow moody and withdrawn, preferring to shut themselves off from family and friends and to opt out of activities they previously enjoyed. The challenges of contemporary family life can further complicate things. In most households nowadays, both parents work, often for very long hours, in order to support their family. And many households are headed by single parents who must cope with working all week while also maintaining the home and tending to their kids' needs. These demands can take a toll on the ability of family members to stay in touch with each other and commonly mean that other individuals—extended family, after-school programming providers, and babysitters—are part of the fabric of a child's life, participating in meal and snack preparation and supervision.

Communicating with teenagers about something as stigmatizing as their intense dieting, binge eating, or purging behavior can be all the more difficult because of the secrecy and shame that accompany eating disorders. So while it is important to talk to your child as soon as you see certain signs and symptoms of an eating disorder appear, it is equally important to do so thoughtfully, calmly, and with advanced preparation. Suspect that your daughter is bulimic? Charging in and yelling things like, "I know you're making yourself throw up and you've got to stop it right now!" will serve no purpose other than to make her react defensively or withdraw from you altogether. It's also likely that she, like many individuals with eating disorders, may be in such denial about her condition that she can't yet acknowledge to herself that her behavior is harmful. Frustrated by your child's difficulty eating flexibly in restaurants or on playdates and wondering if he has ARFID? Screaming in a moment of exasperation, "Enough already! This is the same thing that we serve you at home, it's just made in a different kitchen!" is unlikely to quell anxiety or, most importantly, effect a change in your child's willingness to eat. Yelling and angrily asserting your authority tends to deepen, rather than relieve, a teen's defensive stance. But staying grounded, thinking things through, and planning ahead before you broach the topic with your child will help both of you talk about the situation openly and candidly.

Talking: It's a Good Thing

"Communication was definitely a problem at our house before Vanessa was diagnosed with anorexia nervosa," says Susan. "Both my husband and I worked and had three busy kids who were always on the go. There never seemed to be time to sit down for family meals. Everybody was into his or her own life, and, if we did talk, it was usually while standing around the kitchen eating something on the run. In hindsight, I would make more time for family life and coordinate at least a few family meals. Some kids are likely to resent this at first, but it's important to come together as a family, even if it's only once or twice a week. It gives your kids the message that you care and gives *you* a chance to stop, sit back, and really listen to them."

Preparing Your Approach

One of the first things to do prior to approaching a teenager about his or her eating disorder symptoms is to learn about the illness itself, as well as about weight, exercise, and nutrition. Individuals with eating disorders tend to have skewed ideas about these subjects and are likely to make excuses for their behavior. Arming yourself with information from valid sources will help you to dispel the kind of responses you might get from your son or daughter, such as "I read a magazine article that said I weigh more than I should for how tall I am," "I eat as many calories as I need to. I know because I looked it up and started following someone on Instagram who snaps pictures of her meals and their calorie counts," or "Aunt Shelley said she felt so much better when she went gluten-free."

Some parents have actually had articles, books, and informational websites at the ready for the initial discussion with their children. This can be helpful, but you need to be very careful about the material you ultimately choose. "I knew about eating disorders, of course. When I was a teen, I remember reading about and the struggles of that actress, Tracey Gold, who was on *Growing Pains*. And more recently, there was Portia de Rossi . . . but knowing these people from afar isn't knowing what it was like for them," Jody's mother Shirley explains. "Then, when I started to worry a lot about Jody, I googled 'eating disorders' and found the blog for that National Eating Disorders Association [NEDA]. There were several posts by teens and young adults describing their journeys into and out of illness. I also found a lot of other sites, personal blogs and such, in which people described their journey into bulimic behaviors with graphic details. In one I read, it appeared that a young woman began with the same behaviors I had witnessed in Jody: excessive exercise, counting calories, weighing herself constantly. This was my first reading on bulimia and it scared me."

Shirley emailed the NEDA blog link to Jody with "a gentle note" explaining her concerns. Jody initially replied that Shirley worried needlessly, but later she revealed that the other articles on sites that were less treatment- and recovery-focused, such as the graphic blog Shirley also encountered in her search, had actually given her a lot of specific "how-to's" on bulimia. "I hadn't noticed the many details on specific behaviors the article described," Shirley states. "But they were all Jody had noticed."

The fact is that many articles and books, particularly memoirs written by those who have had anorexia nervosa or bulimia nervosa, tend to be brutally honest about behaviors like purging or laxative abuse. Rather than serving as warnings of the dangers of eating disorders, these descriptions can provide at-risk teens or those who already have eating disorders with provocative tips about dieting and weight loss practices that they haven't yet tried.

If you do consider bringing reading material to your child's attention, we recommend material that has been curated or produced by eating disorder or mental health associations: they purposely avoid describing anything other than signs and symptoms and don't elaborate on behaviors that at-risk teens might be tempted to imitate. They also tend to share a hopeful message about treatment and recovery. You can also consult your pediatrician, family doctor, a school counselor, or a mental health association about appropriate literature that they might recommend. The sites for reputable national organizations with potentially relevant information are listed in the Resources section of this book.

Before approaching your child, also do some research on what local resources and treatment options are available to you and your teen. Again, a professional should be able to provide information and referrals for specialists in your area. They may also be able to help you find local support groups for parents of children with eating disorders. If not, there is support available through online communities such as that of Families Empowered and Supporting Treatment for Eating Disorders's (FEAST) Around the Dinner Table digital forum. And, fortunately, some parents have written extensively about their experiences in the trenches, helping their child through the throes of an eating disorder, including author Harriet Brown in her parenting memoir, *Brave Girl Eating*. Depending on your circumstances, you and your partner may also find it beneficial to initially meet with a therapist before talking to your child so as to allow any expressions of strong emotions or anger to be worked out in advance. If this is not a possibility for you because of time or financial constraints, using a relative or trusted friend as a sounding board might help. They won't be in a position to offer professional advice, but you'll still have an opportunity to vent your frustrations at them rather than at your teen and to role-play so that you get practice expressing your concern clearly and responding to your teen's anticipated reaction.

> Before approaching your child . . . do some research on what local resources and treatment options are available to you and your teen.

Once you're prepared to meet with your son or daughter, pick a moment that is calm (Think: "Strike while the iron is cold!") and a place that's comfortable and familiar—the living room, the child's bedroom, your den—and make sure you allow as much time as you need to talk about the issue thoroughly. This is a tough task you're undertaking. Broaching the subject while driving your teen to school or starting the conversation when there is high likelihood you'll be interrupted will only delay what you hope to accomplish. Starting the conversation when you or teen are exhausted or highly emotional will also likely complicate an already difficult talk. Make sure also that your first discussion is private: the only people present should be you, your spouse or partner, and your teenager. Siblings, grandparents, aunts, uncles, cousins, or friends should not be included as their presence could cause your child to feel under attack or ganged up on, thereby distracting him or her from what you're saying.

The Conversation

When initiating the discussion, first stress how much you love your child and that your concerns stem from that love. It sounds trite, but all teenagers, no matter how grown up they seem, do need to hear this reassurance from you—that you have only their best interests at heart and that you are not the enemy. Be straightforward and direct about what's bothering you about their behavior. Try to remain as calm as possible. The attitude you'd like to convey is that you are concerned, but not panicked, and that, as a parent who loves your child, you are committed to figuring out what is wrong and helping to get it taken care of.

Even though you and your daughter or son might have been very close prior to the development of the eating disorder, it is important for you to be steadfast in your parental role. As Shirley points out, "Jody and I had always been very close. Therefore, I attempted a friendly rather than firm approach, assuming it would make it easier for her to listen and comprehend my heart-to-heart chat. Unfortunately, I didn't realize how involved and distracted her brain was. I thought she was capable of being rational. That was an erroneous assumption on my part. Jody needed a parent, not a friend." Being a parent to your child means you can be authoritative but not dictatorial. You can still be gentle and compassionate while remaining firm in your effort to convince your child that he or she needs your help.

Be steadfast in your parental role.

During your discussion, refrain from using such negative phrases as "You're too skinny," or "Can't you see what you're doing to yourself?" Such an approach can backfire. "I kept thinking that if I could get her to see what she was doing to herself," says one mother whose daughter developed anorexia nervosa, "she'd be able to figure it out and stop losing weight. But

I was wrong. Following a heated confrontation that dissolved into a screaming match, I finally dragged her to a full-length mirror and forced her to look at herself. She was horrified, but not for the same reason I was. What I thought she'd see was the walking skeleton she'd become. However, what she saw was 'a huge, hideous, grotesque, inhuman freak.' Of course, she couldn't explain this to me until after she'd started therapy and her description still haunts me. She's such a beautiful child, and I am still trying to understand why she saw herself as something so horrifying. And even though she's been on the road to recovery for a couple of years now, I wake up every morning praying she'll never have to see herself that way again."

"A huge, hideous, grotesque, inhuman freak"—this is a typical self-image that individuals in the grip of anorexia or bulimia nervosa have. Assume that your daughter, based on the behavior you've observed in her recently, sees herself in much the same way. Do not assume that your son, just because he's a boy, is somehow able to see himself in a better light. He can't at this time see himself as you do, and so try to reach him—to open up a dialogue with him—through personal observations that don't directly challenge this self-image per se but that may help him understand why you're worried. Statements such as "I've noticed that you seem very anxious lately" or "I hear you say you're too fat and that worries me" don't assign blame but instead put the emphasis on you and on what you're feeling about the situation.

If you suspect that your child is experiencing symptoms of binge-eating disorder, it is advisable to focus your first conversation on your concerns about the eating behavior, when and why the binges occur, and overall psychological health, rather than on physical appearance. When she started to notice a lot of food going missing, Theresa remembers gently approaching her daughter, Camilla, by asking why Camilla had started spending so much time alone in her bedroom with the door closed. "It was interesting. When I expressed my concern about Camilla isolating herself, she told me about the problems she was having with some of her friends. And then when I asked her what she was doing in her room when she felt upset, she reluctantly admitted that she was trying to numb out with food. I think it was good that in that first conversation we just focused on her sadness and loneliness and got the binge eating out in the open between us. I don't think it would have gone as well if I'd started the conversation by pointing out that pants I'd bought her two months earlier no longer fit."

Theresa recalls Camilla's initial response to her as one of embarrassment and sadness, but of course this is only one of a range of possible reactions. Andrew remembers that before Zach approached him for help with his ARFID symptoms, every time he tried to sit down and express concern to his son, Zach's anxiety about addressing his food restrictions would make him "beyond irritable and snippy." If your child's initial response is anger or denial, try to stay cool and keep your own emotions in check. If you become angry, it will only convince your teen that you are indeed the enemy—that you're someone who wants to take away the only effective method she or he thinks is available to deal with food, weight, or emotions such as sadness and anxiety. Also, since much shame accompanies eating disorders, your child may be furious with you for discovering their "secret." By remaining calm, you stand a better chance of getting your teen to eventually hear your concerns.

> If your child's initial response is anger or denial, try to stay cool and keep your own emotions in check.

Some children may strategize in an attempt to placate you. Instead of blowing up, they might remain completely cool and try to spin the conversation so as to take the focus off of them. They could say, "Oh, Mom, you always worry too much. I'm fine, really. Actually, I'm worried about *you*. You work too hard. You need to relax. Why don't you go do that right now? I can take care of myself." A good response to that ploy would be to say that, while you'll be very pleased if they are indeed fine, you still want them to go to the doctor, just to be sure.

Whatever the tone of his or her response, your child is likely to resist your initial attempts at offering help. It's true that some children are actually relieved when their parents offer assistance because it means they no longer have to struggle with their eating disorder by themselves, but they are an exception. Many teens, including those who may even be aware they have an eating disorder, are reluctant to want help. Those with anorexia or bulimia nervosa may imagine that treatment is all about being "forced to get fat." Those with binge-eating disorder may feel ashamed of their eating behavior and feel like they can "fix the problem" on their own. Teens with ARFID may feel like their eating patterns work well to quell anxiety and feel that it's unnecessarily scary to confront their fears. You may, in short, need to talk to your child numerous times—patiently but firmly and authoritatively—before he or she begins to accept the notion of getting help.

And you may have to constantly shore up this acceptance once it comes. It may be tentative or short-lived, and you'll likely have to shift between pushing your son or daughter forward to the next step or pulling back and trying to allow the child's own resolve to develop. Parents need not overwhelm their children with the specifics about a treatment plan until the teens can first adjust to the acknowledgment that there is a problem and that professional help will be required for it to be fully addressed. Once they've adjusted to this new reality, they might then be comforted by their parents' effort to find help for them.

Still other teenagers might start out amenable to treatment and then suddenly refuse to go. Their excuse could be that they've decided they don't need a doctor and can stop the disordered eating behavior on their own or that they already *have* stopped. Don't buy these excuses. If you believe your child's behavior continues to show the signs and symptoms of an eating disorder, keep talking, keep pressing your points, but, if need be, it goes without saying, take action and get your child into treatment immediately. It may help for you to see an experienced therapist even without your child to get some guidance about what you can do to help your son or daughter.

The Role of Teachers and Coaches: Communicating with a Student or Athlete Who Has an Eating Disorder

Adolescents spend much of their daily lives in school under the supervision of adults other than their parents, and they can be enormously influenced by anything an authority figure in school says or does. This may be especially true for adolescents at risk of developing eating disorders. Given their tendency to be perfectionistic, they can be deeply affected by what a respected teacher or coach says to them. Whether in the realm of track, basketball, soccer, swimming, dance, drama, or some other activity, negative comments from a coach or a teacher about weight and size can make such a strong impression on adolescent athletes or performers that they may think the only way they can stay on a team or in a class is if they change how they look.

They might even believe they're doing the team or class a favor by becoming smaller. Judith's daughter Katherine was on the soccer team when she started losing a great deal of weight. Judith worried about her because she seemed "so stressed out" and finally talked to her about the weight loss. Her excuse was that she was thinning down to help the team. She told Judith that she was so much faster since she'd lost weight. "Just think how much faster I'll be when I've lost even more," Katherine said.

The desire to excel and to win can be natural, but when overcharged in an impressionable adolescent, it can lead to damaging results. Books like Joan Ryan's *Little Girls in Pretty Boxes* (1995) and Jennifer Sey's *Chalked Up* (2008) describe how the extreme dieting practices of elite athletes such as gymnasts and figure skaters were once encouraged by coaches and teachers. Some Olympic trainers held such unhealthy sway over the lives of young athletes because their methods produced what every country demanded: winners. In other sports as well, some coaches communicated (either verbally or by implication) that the thinner (or sometimes, more muscular) an athlete was, the better shot he or she had at making the team. Similar encouragement for potentially extreme weight loss has also been described in the dance world: the only way for a ballerina to be "in" with a company was to be thin, and dancers even shared tips with each other about how to fast and about the best ways to purge.

Most teachers and coaches now realize the importance of putting more emphasis on health and nutrition rather than on body size. Communicating such values to young athletes can help them stay healthy and active in both the short and long terms. In addition, a coach or instructor who doesn't attach a stigma to weight can do a lot to raise an adolescent's self-esteem. Candy, who is now an adult but who as a teenager struggled with binge eating that led to obesity, talks about how her high-school P.E. teacher helped her.

"I started getting really fat when I hit puberty. By the time I turned 15, I weighed 200 pounds. There were a lot of problems at home, I was really depressed, and kept eating everything in sight. But I also loved sports and my ninth-grade Phys Ed teacher was terrific. First, she made me a part of the team that was entered in a local gymnastics' exhibition. I remember thinking 'Is she out of her mind?' because I knew I'd be the biggest girl there and would surely cause us to lose. Well, we didn't win, but I did the best double rolls of anybody thanks to her. She also put me on our school's relay track team that was entered in an all-city tournament. All the other teams looked so smug when I lined up because I'm sure they thought '*That* girl can't beat us,' but we actually won the meet. And then, to everybody's shock, Mrs. Morrison made me first string on the basketball team. We wound up winning another all-city tournament, and I received an award for having the highest rebound total. While it took me years to learn what my triggers were for binge eating and to then establish and maintain a healthy weight for myself, I'm still grateful to Mrs. Morrison for seeing me as the person I was rather than just another 'fat kid.' Attitude is everything and hers changed my life."

Providing positive reinforcement can certainly help an at-risk adolescent, but teachers and coaches who suspect that a student or a team member of theirs has an eating disorder can help in other ways as well. The NEDA offers downloadable toolkits for educators as well as for coaches and trainings (see Resources section). Teachers and coaches can

- Talk directly to the student, making sure they're prepared before starting the discussion by learning as much as they can about eating disorders and about what relevant resources might be available to the student at the school or in the community.
- Find out about school policy regarding students with eating disorders and how it might affect his or her participation in classes and sports.
- Use a quiet, private place for their conversation with the student so that his or her confidentiality is maintained and allow enough time for the talk to occur without interruption.
- Share their concerns in a manner that conveys personal regard for the teen as a unique individual rather than as just somebody else in class or on the team and that are cast as observations rather than as judgments: for example, "You don't seem to be enjoying the class as much as you used to," or "I'm worried that you might be doing more harm than good with those extra-long workouts."
- Directly and nonjudgmentally share specific observations of behaviors you have witnessed or heard about from the teen's peers that concern you.
- Anticipate the likelihood that the student may deny he or she has a problem but avoid a battle of wills likely to upset the student. If things get too heated, it's best to end the conversation and try approaching the student again later.
- Have some resources and referrals available to give to the student in the event he or she accepts the need for help.

- Plan for a follow-up conversation. While your responsibility is not to diagnose or provide therapy, it is to help a student in trouble with compassion, support, and appropriate resources for evaluation and clinical care.
- Seek professional help immediately if the student is in a life-threatening situation (i.e., is passing out in class or seems suicidal or depressed).

Coaches can support a healthy team culture by deemphasizing weight (e.g., not weighing athletes, eliminating derogatory comments about weight and body size or shape) and challenging the assumption that reducing body fat or weight categorically improves performance. Instead, coaches can help teens enhance their performance by focusing on strength, physical conditioning, and psychological adaptability in competition.

Teachers, coaches, and other school personnel alike must maintain meaningful communication not only with each other about a student's behavior at school but most especially with the student's parents. As Bobbie, whose daughter was diagnosed with anorexia nervosa, states, "My daughter Sarah was throwing away the lunches I made for her every day to take to school because, as she told me later, after she was in treatment, she knew she couldn't be the smartest or the prettiest, but at least wanted to try to be the smallest. But because she wasn't eating, she eventually passed out in chorus class and was sent to the school nurse, who did nothing more than accept her excuse about why she'd fainted ('It was so hot in that room and I was standing on a riser'). Well, I had no idea my kid had passed out in school because nobody told me—not the teacher, not the nurse, nobody. Why one of them didn't call me or talk to me, I'll never know, but it's obvious they weren't talking to each other either. That's why I think schools need to set protocols. Each person, whether it's a teacher, school nurse, counselor, or principal, all need to bring a piece of the puzzle to complete the whole picture that parents can't fill in by themselves."

"I had no idea my kid had passed out in school because nobody told me—not the teacher, not the nurse, nobody."

Treatment and Recovery: Staying the Course, Staying Strong, Staying in Touch

Entering and sticking with a treatment program for a serious illness, including an eating disorder, can be a daunting prospect for anyone. It can be especially so for an adolescent. Some teens can be frightened at the thought of being turned over to strangers, especially if hospitalization is required. Certain outpatient approaches, including family-based therapy (described in Chapter 3), will require that parents play a role in meal preparation and supervision that would otherwise be developmentally inappropriate for an adolescent, and some teens may find this embarrassing or angering. Therefore, it is very important for you as a parent to reassure your daughter or son of your continuing emotional support during the treatment process and your sincere wish that the hard work they are doing will allow them to be in charge of their choices (rather than you, or the eating disorder) in the future. Knowing of your enduring support can make a big difference in your child's attitude about spending time away from home (if hospitalized) or about outpatient therapy.

It is also important to let the treatment run its course, even if you see your child making good progress early on, and to seek the judgment of his or her doctor or therapist as to when treatment can conclude. Your resolve may sometimes be heart-wrenchingly difficult to sustain: "The greatest strain of visiting her," says Valerie, whose daughter Audra was hospitalized for anorexia nervosa, "wasn't the 8-hour car trip it took to get there but having to be strong when she begged and pleaded with us to take her home."

Sometimes, a good treatment outcome sets the stage for new challenges. "My wife and I were so happy when Zach was finally willing to work on eating more flexibly and by the time he graduated from high school, he'd had a lot of successes," his father, Andrew, remembers. "Exposure sessions helped Zach so much. It was easier for him to eat out with his friends, and he was buying lunch a few days a week at the cafeteria to practice what it would be like in college. And I was getting better at managing my own anxiety about the whole thing but still, I was pretty worried about what would happen when Zach went away to school." Life transitions, such as the transition from high school to college, do present unique challenges for adolescents with eating disorders. Responsibility for portioning, differences in the array of available foods than at home, and ever-changing class schedules can create a context for a return to restrictive eating. Changes in sleeping patterns, substance use, and food availability can, for the vulnerable teen, increase risks of binge eating.

> Life transitions . . . present unique challenges for adolescents with eating disorders.

Your ultimate commitment is to your son's or daughter's long-term recovery and health, not to their assurances that they've recovered or even to intermediate marks of progress

that you yourself see. Talk with your child's treatment provider routinely about those marks and assess their significance
together and in light of the provider's expertise. In anticipation of life transitions such as starting college (or graduating
college and living independently), have a frank conversation
with your child about how they are doing, anything you or
they are worried about going forward, and whether arrang-
ing ongoing treatment in a new place might be helpful. Even
when it seems that regular outpatient therapy is not necessary,
parental support likely will be. This might come in the form
of helping with a grocery budget, accompanying your child
when he or she goes shopping for work clothes, and assisting
your child in establishing care with a primary care physician
for annual visits.

For many teenagers, the battle to overcome an eating disorder can remain a struggle even after a course of treatment.
It can be equally stressful for parents, relatives, friends, and
other people in the teen's life. The following are two stories
exemplifying different kinds of ups and downs that parents
can experience with a teen with an eating disorder.

Carlos and Adriana's Story

After the diagnosis of anorexia nervosa was established, Carlos
and Adriana and their daughter Cristina started seeing a therapist who specialized in family-based treatment for eating disorders. According to Adriana, the therapy helped "somewhat."
It got her and Carlos "out of denial and informed" about
Cristina's condition and how crucial renourishment was to
her physical and psychological health. "When we took charge
of when and what she was eating, it initially worked," Carlos
remembers. "But," he adds, "it was an incredible strain on
Adriana and me. It was exhausting, and once Cristina gained

a little weight and had more energy, she also became more fearful of the process, of getting fat, and more resistant to our efforts." Adriana adds, "After that initial improvement, it did get way harder. Cristina would curse at us, try to lock herself in her room, and threaten that she would hurt herself if we kept insisting that she eat. It was scary and painful to witness, and we were also worried about the impact her behavior was having on her younger sister, Maya." Cristina started to lose weight again and became suicidal.

"She took over-the-counter medications like Benadryl and Tylenol PM by the handful to try to kill herself, then she'd sit in our family sessions and smile smugly, telling us she was fine. We knew she wasn't, and, if she had taken an overdose or when we were scared she was going to hurt herself, we'd have to take her to the emergency room. Finally, we got tired of the cycle and had to get her into a more intensive treatment." After a few months, Adriana and Carlos eventually secured a spot for Cristina in a residential eating disorders program that had a program for adolescents, and, once there, her daughter became a model patient. The program was far away, but either Adriana or Carlos drove there to visit her every day. After only 2 weeks, Cristina told Adriana she was cured and "good to go."

"That was the beginning of 2 years of hell," Carlos says. "When she got home, she went right back to her old habits of not eating, losing weight, and overdosing on pills. Her problems became the focus of our entire life. It was just so weird because, before the eating disorder, Cristina was the absolute best kid. She got along great with her little sister, she never got into any trouble, she excelled academically, had lots of friends, and was invited to become a member of any club she wanted to join. Then, practically within the blink of an eye, everything changed, and Cristina became someone I couldn't even recognize. I kept asking myself how we could've let it happen. I kept thinking that somehow I'd failed as a person and, most importantly, as a father."

> "Her problems became the focus of my entire life."

"My own sister was bulimic for a while in college," adds Adriana, "so I had a little bit of experience with trying to understand the mind of someone with an eating disorder. But I guess her problem was not so severe. She went to therapy for a few months, stopped binge eating and purging, and besides feeling a little more unhappy with her body than other people, she was pretty much okay. What was going on with Cristina was a whole other level." With erratic behavior, tremendous mood swings, and more suicide attempts, Cristina dictated the household, particularly around food issues.

"She was always telling us what we could and couldn't eat, and, if we bought something she didn't want us to have, she'd throw it out in the middle of the night. Nights were when her demons came out and that made it very hard for the rest of us," recalls Adriana. "We'd get up in the morning never knowing what we'd find. One morning was particularly frightening. I walked into her bedroom to wake her up and found it completely destroyed. She had scrawled 'I hate myself' all over the walls, and, for the first time, I really felt all of her hatred, anger, and pain. I was terrified and searched for her everywhere. I finally found her down in the basement. She was asleep. When I woke her, she just smiled up at me and said, 'Hi, Mom. Guess you could tell I had a bad night, huh?'"

As much as Cristina's parents empathized with their daughter, they could also see how much Cristina's out-of-control behavior was affecting the family and, in particular, her younger sister.

"We finally came to the conclusion that there was no other choice but to try some tough love. We tried to do it as firmly as possible to let her know we weren't going to back down. We'd already given in to her too many times, and it obviously hadn't helped at all. We told her we desperately needed to restore order in the household by setting up some rules. We left it up to her to either conform to our terms or leave. She chose to leave, which broke our hearts, but we had to stand by what we'd said." Cristina wound up moving in with her friend Brenda but was kicked out shortly after she arrived.

"We got a call from Brenda's mother, who told us that Cristina's mood swings and wild behavior were distracting Brenda, who was a scholarship student and had to keep her grades up," says Carlos. Although they didn't know it at the time, Cristina had also started binge eating and was eating Brenda out of house and home. "We had to call Cristina and tell her that since another family was now involved, she needed to either go back into a program or come home. She refused, saying she'd met a boy and would move in with him. That didn't last long either because she wound up in an intensive care unit after overdosing on a combination of prescription antidepressants and sleeping pills. When we arrived at the hospital, she was in pretty bad shape physically and mentally."

Fortunately, Cristina survived this crisis and in time she did turn a corner to accept the fact that she needed help. "I'm still trying to put all the pieces of the puzzle together and understand what turned things around for her," Adriana says, "and there's still a lot of work to be done, but we're getting there." Cristina continues to struggle with the effects of her eating disorder on a daily basis. She is still underweight, has chronic stomach problems, and has trouble moving her bowels because of laxative abuse.

"But the upside," Carlos says, "is that Cristina has started to embrace life again. She eventually wants to finish college and become a nutritionist so she can help other people with eating disorders. She has watched her younger sister build a full life and wants to be a good aunt for her young nephew. I sometimes wonder if she'd ever even be able to physically have a child of her own. If she completes her education, enters a profession, and develops a healthy romantic relationship one day, we'll be thrilled, but for right now, we are honestly just grateful she is alive."

Dana's Story

"Lily's eating problem—ARFID—started when she was 13, but it took another year and a half until we had a proper diagnosis," recalls her mother, Dana. Along the way, as medical workups were pursued to get to the bottom of Lily's stomach complaints, Dana had suspected something psychological was going on. Lily even saw a supportive psychotherapist for a while, and, according to Dana, "it was helpful in the sense that she could talk about things that were bothering her, but at the end of the day, she was still missing out socially and losing weight because she was too petrified of choking or of becoming nauseous to eat normally.

"It was when we got ourselves in for a consultation with an eating disorders specialist, at our pediatrician's suggestion, that we really began to see what Lily needed to work on, and how. Lily was pretty scared of tackling her fears head on in exposure therapy sessions, but she really wanted to be able to do things her friends were doing, like go the beach for the weekend with someone else's family." Given the nature of her eating disorder, gaining weight was not in and of itself aversive to Lily. Instead, she was motivated to be able to fit into her favorite jeans again, to get taller, and, in her words, "maybe get some curves like the other girls in my grade."

Being highly motivated did not make the treatment easy, however. "Lily was so scared to do the things her therapist was asking of her, and it was really unsettling for me as a parent to see her in such distress. Plus, some of the exposures were so weird. I mean, spinning in a chair a bunch of times and then drinking lemonade, or eating a huge handful of dry pretzels in one bite without being able to wash it down with water: who would want to do that?" Dana tried to remember for herself, and to constantly remind her daughter, that "the only way for it to get less scary is to do weird, hard stuff and realize nothing bad will happen and that you can handle it." Dana and Lily worked together with the therapist to identify motivating rewards for Lily whenever she took a big stride toward overcoming her fears. Along the way, Lily's efforts "earned her rights as movie selection decision-maker for family Netflix night, a manicure, a rock-climbing lesson, and eventually even a new iPhone!"

After approximately 6 months of weekly exposure therapy sessions, Lily's weight was out of the danger zone and she was growing again. Her eating was more varied, and, most importantly, in her words, "I got the hang of the whole exposure thing." She stayed in therapy but saw her therapist every other week for a while, and then once a month. "I helped Lily keep track of her progress in between appointments and even coached her through some of the more challenging things she wanted to try if it seemed like she needed my support," recalls Dana. "When she finally went on her first sleepover since this whole thing started, I was on standby for text support and sent her a few messages of encouragement throughout the night, reminding her that if she could eat after spinning round and round in a chair for a minute, then she could definitely handle whatever would be coming her way!"

By the end of her sophomore year in high school, Lily was no longer in specialized treatment, but she did continue to see her pediatrician every few months to check her weight and nutritional status and for the doctor to do a brief assessment of how she was doing with dietary variety. "Now we are approaching the college transition. On the one hand, I'm so proud of my kid for getting herself to the place where she wants and is able to go to school far away from home. On the other hand, I'm concerned that there won't be enough familiarity in the foods in the dining hall," says Dana. "We recently decided to reach back out to Lily's old exposure therapist so that she can go for a few sessions before she leaves for college. Maybe there are some things for them to practice together that we haven't thought of, or some planning to be done, and we can also get a referral for someone near her school in case we need it."

Managing Daily Life

There are no "sure-fire fixes" for eating disorders. As the previous stories indicate, recovering from them may involve some trial-and-error with different types of treatment and can sometimes take a long time. In some cases, it involves relapses. Indeed, more research is needed not only on the causes of eating disorders but also on the triggering events or coexisting conditions that can plunge someone in recovery back into disordered eating habits. Nevertheless, there are many things that parents can do to help their children on a day-to-day basis. As Vanessa's mother Susan says, "We as parents are powerless to 'fix' our children, but we're not powerless in the choices we make to try to help them."

The first step is to recognize that your child's hospitalization or outpatient treatment was a beginning, not an end in itself. Your child has not been "cured" of the disorder but has simply become strong enough because of initial treatment to at least begin navigating daily life again at home and school. The second step is to recognize that a child's recovery can be especially difficult during this reentry period and may require as much vigilance, patience, and assistance from everyone—family, teachers, coaches, and so on—as when the problem was first recognized.

> "We as parents are powerless to 'fix' our children, but we're not powerless in the choices we make to try to help them."

Tips at Home

The havoc that an eating disorder can wreak not only on affected adolescents but also on their families cannot be overstated. If that has been the case for your family, it may be helpful to convene a meeting of sorts—in short, talk to each other, both individually and as a family, about what has happened in your shared lives. Doing so will help reestablish family connections and defuse tensions, for the teenager with the disorder as well as for everyone else involved. Siblings can be deeply affected by a sister's or brother's behavior, for example, and they may feel forgotten or abandoned because you've had to focus so much on the child with the illness. If so, try to reassure them that every member of the household is equally important and encourage them to express their feelings.

Siblings . . . may feel forgotten or abandoned because you've had to focus so much on the child with the illness.

As Carlos and Adriana's story illustrates, limits need to be set within the family framework for a teen who has either just returned home from a structured treatment setting (e.g., a hospital or residential program) or is being treated as an outpatient. Avoiding all discussions and confrontations for fear of precipitating a relapse may actually allow your teen the freedom of falling back into old eating-disordered habits. Conversely, you shouldn't feel you have to constantly police your child. Striking a balance between allowing your teen independence and setting limits on his or her behavior is ideal, but a fine line to tread. If you have a problem with how to respond to your child's needs and behavior, talk to the therapist or treatment team for suggestions about the best approaches you can take and how to set limits on behavior that is likely to disrupt the entire household.

Aspects of daily family life and the way in which family members interact with each other will likely need adjustment as well. Take, for example, mealtimes. These of course can be extremely stressful for teens recovering from an eating disorder. They may have become so obsessed with counting calories and carbohydrates and fat grams that even a single bite of food still terrifies them. They may experience seemingly unbearable urges to purge if feeling very full or if eating a food that they associated with binge eating. They may find the texture of a food highly aversive or be fearful of choking. They are also very aware that everybody in the family knows they have "food issues" and is undoubtedly watching to see what they eat. For that reason, it's best to keep family mealtimes as relaxed as possible (easier said than done, we understand). At meals, families can talk about local events or sports rather than what each family member is eating to help ease tensions about food.

Planning meals in advance can also help reduce mealtime stress. Those in the throes of an eating disorder like anorexia nervosa systematically eliminate foods from their diets until they are only eating things that are extremely low in calories and fat (e.g., lettuce, celery, carrots). It is also not unusual for individuals with bulimia nervosa and some with binge-eating disorder to eat fairly restrictively outside of binge episodes. During recovery, therefore, it is important to help them expand their list of "safe foods." In family-based treatment for anorexia nervosa, your therapist will help you and your partner use data on your child's weight trajectory to understand what increases in intake must be made, when, and how (based on your intuition and your family's eating patterns). As part of meal planning in certain phases and types of treatment, you and your child may be advised to go grocery shopping together and set a goal of buying one new food to try each week or every other week. If your child is undergoing nutritional counseling, ask the nutritionist's advice about which new foods might be good additions to your menu. If your child is doing exposures in his or her outpatient therapy, discuss with the clinician what foods are required for between-session practice. Meal planning in anticipation of meals outside of the home environment—school lunches, overnight excursions, etc.—is a component of eating disorders treatment as well.

> Planning meals in advance can also help reduce mealtime stress.

Cooking and trying out new recipes together are other ways of making food issues less stressful. Do not, however, allow the teen to shop or cook for the family by him- or herself unless this is a goal established in consultation with a treatment provider (as it often is in latter phases of treatment). Many people with eating disorders will feed their families as a way to avoid feeding themselves. By cooking, serving, and then not eating the food they've prepared, they are proving that they are in control of the food rather than the food controlling them. The meals they serve can be elaborate and take all day for them to prepare. They may also make a point of serving all the favorite foods they used to eat and of then watching vicariously as their family eats them. If asked why they're not joining the family for such a scrumptious meal, they may say that they did a lot of tasting while making the dish or that they ate a big helping before bringing it to the table. If you and your child cook the meal together, you can then observe how much he or she actually eats.

The physical changes, such as weight gain, that are brought about by treatment for disorders such as anorexia nervosa and atypical anorexia nervosa can also cause stress. With the notable exception of ARFID, individuals with eating disorders tend to be quite concerned about being or becoming overweight. Even in recovery, it may still take a while to come to grips with the return to a healthier, balanced lifestyle and whatever weight and body shape is associated with that. Therefore, it's wise to avoid saying things like "You look so much better since you put on weight," or "I'm so proud of you for putting on a few pounds." Such comments, while well-meaning, might cause them to panic because they think, "Oh my god, if they keep making me eat, I'm going to be a blimp! I've got to start losing weight again right now!" Instead, comment positively on changes you've noticed in your child as a person rather than in his or her physical appearance. You might notice, for example, that your teen's mood seems better, that he or she is smiling more. In time, of course, your teen's recovery will involve learning how to more accurately hear positive feedback on appearance. In fact, the complete absence of comments about appearance can result in a patient thinking that her or his parents are not offering compliments because they are indeed "fat" or "gross." Therefore, if the dress, or the suit, fits and looks nice by all means it is OK to say "you look great!" on occasion. Striking the right balance isn't easy, and missteps are to be expected and, ideally, openly discussed.

Teenagers in recovery from eating disorders may feel overwhelmed or suffocated by all the attention, at home or in individual and family-based therapy sessions, that is focused on them, their eating habits, and their interpersonal relationships. Siblings may wind up feeling neglected and resentful of their sister or brother. You might intentionally redirect parental attention to the unaffected sibling(s) when crisis moments have passed. Be sure to give your affected child a breather from this attention and do things together that don't revolve around food or weight issues. Invite your son to go to a movie with you, or check out the latest exhibition at a local museum with your daughter. Or just window-shop. If the doctor certifies that your child is physically strong enough, you might suggest a day trip to a favorite getaway spot. As he or she continues to recover, talk to the child's treatment team about scheduling more activities for just the two of you or with the entire family. These will help you to develop and maintain a relationship with your child that is not focused on his or her having an eating disorder.

Earlier in this discussion, Susan spoke of the fact that parents can do a lot to assist their children's recovery from an eating disorder. They can indeed, and so can whole families. As the foregoing suggests, that help can come in the form of changing family life so that it adequately supports the child's treatment and recovery process. The process will likely have some rocky moments along the way, but one of the signs it's going well is when you begin to see your child help him- or herself in truly positive ways.

Susan again: "Before the eating disorder, Vanessa was always the peacemaker in the family. Whenever there was a conflict, she'd step in and calm everybody down. It was a great gift, but when I look back on it, I wonder just how much of herself she was suppressing to keep peace in our home. Since entering therapy, however, she has become much more assertive and now fights with her brother and sister the way most siblings do. Most people with eating disorders use the fact that they're not eating to tell you there's something wrong. They're also in such deep denial that they really don't want to listen to anything you have to say. The fact that she's finally able to talk to everyone and advocate for herself is wonderful."

TIPS AT SCHOOL

Returning to school after a hospitalization or a stay at a residential program can be enormously difficult for adolescents with an eating disorder. They may wonder what their peers know about their absence, or they may worry that they've been a subject of gossip. How they choose to navigate their return—for example, how they respond to questions and concerns about why they were gone or what made them sick—is entirely up to them. Likely they'll be torn about what to do or say. If they choose to share their dilemma with you, you can help by listening and, if you feel it's appropriate, by offering some suggestions. However, if they don't ask for your help or reject your suggestions, don't force the issue or push your point by saying something like "Well, I think you'd feel better if you told so-and-so. After all, you were best friends before all this happened." Some teens might be more comfortable talking to a trusted teacher, coach, or counselor with both knowledge of the eating disorder and enough savvy about the teens' particular peer group to be a good sounding board or to offer good advice.

And some teens decide on their own what they do and don't want others to know, and take reentry into school life as it comes. "When my son Michael was hospitalized, his friends and professors were awesome," says Diane. "They were so supportive of him just getting well. However, he did not want anyone to know he had an eating disorder, and I do think if his friends knew he had anorexia nervosa, they may have treated him differently. It was interesting because, after taking a leave from college for a semester, during his second week back, one of his friends asked him, 'What was wrong with you?' Michael told him that life had just gotten to be too much for him, that he was really stressed out, and lost a lot of weight. His friend said, 'Oh, that happened to me, too, but my grades just went down.' How great is that? So simple, yet so complicated."

Still, a student returning to the classroom does present certain challenges, such that reentry can be made easier if you forge a partnership with school personnel and teachers and then routinely stay in touch with them about your child's progress. Some teachers may worry that they have to treat the teen differently from the rest of the class. As the teen's parent, you should urge them to avoid paying undue attention that can embarrass your child—who's already self-conscious enough after all—or that may send the wrong message: that attention is based on appearance. At the same time, because hospitalization or even outpatient treatment can cause some adolescents with eating disorders to fall behind the rest of the class, a teacher might be tempted to assign extra work so that they can catch up. Even if the teen requests extra work—and this is possible, given that most adolescents with eating disorders tend to be overachievers who pride themselves on succeeding academically—an accelerated program may not be a good solution. The effects of eating disorders can be severe, and recovery from them takes time. Since the adolescent's energy and concentration may not yet have returned to the same levels they once were, he or she could be overwhelmed by the pressure of completing more than the regular workload. Instead, you should urge your teen's teachers to focus on how far along he or she is in the course material rather than on where the entire class is and to work with you and your child's treatment team to develop a reasonable, well-paced plan for helping him or her to eventually achieve academic goals.

Adolescents in recovery from an eating disorder may have a special meal plan that requires nutritious snacks and/or a fairly routinized timing of meals to help stave off urges to binge and purge. Here, too, you should work with the school to ensure that your child is given the time to take these, but also to be aware of signs that your teen may be relapsing, such as suddenly eating lots of junk food or bolting for the bathroom after lunch.

Sarah's mother Bobbie emphasizes the critical importance of this communication between school personnel and families.

"I think it's key to watch for anything our children seem to be struggling with, whether it's eating, drinking, drugs, or whatever else might be bothering them. They are all part of our society and have problems coping just like adults. The goal is to raise a healthy, happy, self-confident child. Anything that gets in the way of that is a problem you have to deal with, and deal with it as soon as you possibly can, because the longer it goes on, the harder it is to change. This can only come by communicating with your child as well as the people they spend time with. I think that catching Sarah's problem early made all the difference in how well she's recovered. She's doing so great that it almost seems like a lifetime ago when we had to rush her to the ER because she'd fainted in the bathroom at home, which was our catalyst for starting family-based therapy. She is now captain of the cheerleading squad, and I am so proud of her. Her coach has been very supportive, has kept an eye on her all season, and has also made a point of incorporating eating plans into her program, not just for Sarah but for all the girls when they are at all-day cheer competitions. It's so great because everybody involved wants to make sure Sarah stays strong and healthy, and, by checking in with each other, we seem to be doing that."

"The goal is to raise a healthy, happy, self-confident child."

Finding Support from Other Parents

Most parents of an adolescent with an eating disorder express the need for support from other parents who were dealing with or have dealt with similar situations. As Michael's mother Diane said, "The greatest help is support from other families. It's absolutely crucial. Eating disorders are family diseases. From Sunday mealtime to every other part of daily life, it all changes, and families need to know that they're not alone."

"Eating disorders are family diseases."

Indeed, families with the same experiences you're facing now can be a source of not only emotional support but also of practical tips and other information that can help you cope with your child's disorder. The problem is that finding such support locally, which is ideal, might not be easy. "In 1999, my parents could not have found any other parents nearby to talk to," says Julian, now an adult recovered from bulimia nervosa. "There weren't the number of websites and other resources devoted to eating disorders that there are now. I understand that now there are whole organizations dedicated to bringing parents together to help one another, either in-person or online. Mostly my folks wound up doing a lot of reading, which helped them understand what I was going through a little, I guess, but I really think they might have been able to help me more if they'd had a one-on-one conversation with somebody who was going through or who had been through what they were going through. As a parent myself now, I feel like even just a little understanding can go a long way to help someone who feels overwhelmed by their parenting situation."

Due to issues of privacy and confidentiality, doctors are restricted in the kind of information they can and can't share about their patients. They might be able to obtain another parent's consent so that you can talk to him or her, but your best bet is to try to find an existing support group for parents of children with eating disorders or to avail yourself of digital resources, such as Around the Dinner Table (a Q & A forum organized by FEAST's online community; see Resources section for more details). "Even though we didn't know anyone else going through what we were going through with Cristina," her mother, Adriana, recalls, "Carlos and I found it very helpful to watch this documentary by Parents to Parents about what parents of kids with anorexia nervosa wish they had understood from the start. We felt less alone, and it helped us begin to separate our daughter from what the illness was doing to our daughter." The link to the documentary to which Adriana refers can be found in the Resources section at the end of this book.

Fortunately, as studies have supported the use of family-based therapy for eating disorders specifically and parental involvement in general, the landscape of in-person parental support is much less bleak than it was when Julian's parents were trying to help him with his bulimic symptoms. Some outpatient, intensive outpatient, residential, and hospital programs offer multifamily groups as a routine part of treatment. In these groups, parents and teens come together to learn from one another about the disorders and how families in the trenches are fighting back.

When Michael was in treatment for anorexia nervosa, he and Diane participated in multifamily groups, and she was very relieved to learn that what she and Michael were going through was par for the course with the disorder.

"The first time I went, it was so great," she says. "The people there were totally supportive, and I was able to share things with them that I couldn't talk to other people about, and we could exchange ideas based on what had been helpful for us and our kids along the way. It was also useful to meet other kids having a similar experience to Michael. Sometimes it was easier to talk to them than my own son about the anorexic mindset. Somehow, I felt less angry and more determined to help him beat this thing."

As Cristina's illness and treatment course wound up being extended, Adriana and Carlos eventually found a general parent support group in their area. Carlos was reluctant to go, but Adriana eagerly went to check it out. Then there was an unexpected problem when Cristina found out that Adriana was going to the group. "She became furious with me for talking about her to strangers and screamed at me, 'This isn't your stuff, this is *my* stuff.' I was so taken aback by her anger that I was tempted to tell her I wouldn't go anymore. She was in such a fragile state—both physically and emotionally—and I didn't want to risk upsetting her further. Then I realized that if I didn't do a few things to take care of myself, I'd be no use to her anyway. I'd be letting the disease control me the same way it was controlling Cristina, so I finally told her, 'Look, this isn't just about you anymore. Those of us who care about you are involved, too. If you want to stay mad at me, fine, go right ahead, but right now I need help, too.'"

If, after exhausting all online and local channels, you're still unable to connect with other parents and feel an in-person group would be especially beneficial, you might consider starting a support group yourself. That prospect may seem daunting at first, especially if you're trying to juggle work responsibilities, home life, therapy sessions, or hospital visits. If so, think about asking a family member or friend to lend a hand. Lots of people who care about you and your family would probably feel pleased you asked and would be eager to help. They could even assist you in solving some logistical problems, such as where to hold your meetings, and go with you to check out the possibilities. Local businesses, schools, churches, or other organizations might be willing to allow you to use their space or offer to put the word out about your group. Another way to reach potential group members is to place an ad online for popular local parenting, school, or town publications. Numerous free newspapers and magazines are distributed in neighborhoods around the country, and most of them have "Community Events" sections where people can place ads for free (or a nominal fee) if you're not charging admission for your event. You could also print up support group meeting fliers and post them anywhere you're allowed to, such as in libraries, laundromats, supermarkets, bookstores, or local bulletin boards.

Many colleges and universities also have programs on eating disorders. If there is a campus nearby, talk to an administrator or instructor there about making contact with other parents or ask about any support services they offer.

If all else fails, contact the numerous organizations around the country for information, support services, and professional referrals. Their names, phone numbers, and websites are listed in the Resources section of this book.

Chapter Five

Preventing Eating Disorders

Parents have reason to be optimistic about the outcome of a child with an eating disorder: most adolescents with an eating disorder do, in fact, recover. However, the treatments currently available are not as effective or rapid as parents and professionals would like, and some youngsters suffer for a long time. It is critically important that the search continue for more precise and useful definitions of eating disorders and for improved methods to treat them. An even more desirable goal would be to mount an effective effort to prevent their occurrence in the first place by targeting young children and adolescents who may be most at risk for these illnesses.

> Most adolescents with an eating disorder do, in fact, recover.

Michael's mother Diane highlights the need for effective prevention. "Back in the 1930s and '40s, teenagers started smoking cigarettes because they thought it was the cool thing to do. At that point, there were no studies about the harmful effects of smoking tobacco. But now we know better and warn our kids about how hazardous smoking is. There have also been effective ad campaigns aimed at kids to show them the dangers of drinking alcohol and using drugs like ecstasy, cocaine, and heroin. So why are we not warning the group at highest risk for developing eating disorders—our teenagers—about how physically damaging and deadly these syndromes can be?"

Jody's mother Shirley further notes that the only time the media ever pays attention to eating disorders is if a celebrity is involved, like when Portia de Rossi disclosed her anorexia nervosa, when Princess Diana admitted she was bulimic, or, more recently, when Lady Gaga, Lily Collins, and Gabourey Sidibe spoke frankly about their eating disorder histories.

"It's not enough for the press that ordinary people struggle with these diseases every day," she says. "There always has to be a famous name attached before a story about eating disorders is deemed newsworthy, and that's just not right. We need stories that reflect the realities of the disorders as well as ad blitzes along the lines of 'Friends Don't Let Friends Drive Drunk' to reach our kids before it's too late."

Chelsey's mother Donna adds, "Prevention efforts need to start in schools when kids are very young. Teaching self-esteem is the key. Children need to be taught to value themselves for who they are and for all of their talents. Dieting is starting younger and younger these days. A friend of mine who is an elementary school teacher told me that girls in her third-grade class have brought cans of Slim-Fast to school for lunch. When my friend asked one of the students if her parents were aware that she was only having a diet drink for lunch, the little girl replied, 'Oh, sure. My mom's the one who gave it to me.' It's shocking. These kids are only 7 or 8 years old, they aren't even fully grown yet, and their parents are already filling their heads with the wrong ideas. I think all parents, and young mothers and fathers in particular, need to learn about nutrition and healthy lifestyle habits."

"Children need to be taught to value themselves for who they are and for all of their talents."

However, while very appealing to parents and professionals, the goal of preventing eating disorders is elusive. Certainly, educating the public about eating disorders and increasing broad public awareness—on the part not only of parents and children but also of teachers, counselors, and even medical professionals, such as pediatricians, adolescent medicine doctors, or other primary care physicians who may come into contact with young at-risk patients—of the dangers of these diseases can play a key role in their recognition and in preventing the first symptoms from turning into a full-blown disorder. At the same time, a vital component of the effort to prevent any disorder is a firm understanding of the risk factors that may contribute to its development. But in the case of eating disorders, that understanding is incomplete.

As discussed in Chapter 2, the causes of eating disorders involve a mix of biological, environmental, psychological, and social factors whose exact contribution to the development of these disorders is not yet fully understood and that likely vary across the disorders and among the individuals who develop them. To educate the public about the dangers of these disorders is one thing, but to effectively prevent their occurrence, especially in light of the limited knowledge about their risk factors, is a much taller order. The programs that have been launched in an effort to prevent or at least reduce the occurrence of these disorders or their symptoms have been based on reasonable assumptions about dieting, body image, low self-esteem, and other elements implicated in the development of eating disorders, not on actual known truths about them. Nonetheless, some of these programs have shown promising results, and researchers continue to improve them. This chapter examines some of the prevention approaches that have been tried, explores the controversial topic of whether treating obesity might be viewed as a risk factor for eating disorders, and offers tips on what parents and others can do themselves to help prevent eating disorders in children and adolescents.

Prevention Approaches

Two prevention approaches— "universal" and "targeted"— have been used to try to reduce the incidence of eating disorders. A *universal prevention program* is one that is applied to an entire group of people and is designed to prevent a disease before it begins by changing, at the group-wide level, the beliefs, attitudes, intentions, and behaviors associated with the occurrence of that disease. For example, people who smoke, eat a diet of foods primarily high in fat and calories, and don't exercise are at increased risk of developing coronary heart disease (CHD). Universal prevention programs for CHD provide education about the dangers of the disease as well as about the harmful effects of smoking, the benefits of eating well-balanced meals, and the need for moderate exercise regimens. In fact, although CHD remains the single leading cause of death in the United States, the mortality rate from CHD has declined substantially in the past few decades, in part because of such prevention efforts.

Similarly, structured, universal prevention approaches for eating disorders focus on an entire population, such as all the students in a high school or junior high school, to promote healthy weight regulation, discourage overly-restrictive dieting (e.g., "crash" diets), and address the ways in which body image and eating are influenced by developmental, social, and cultural factors. Some universal prevention programs focus on broader issues, such as increasing self-esteem and social competence. By contrast, a targeted prevention program is one that tries to identify those individuals who are at high risk of developing eating disorders or who have already begun to exhibit symptoms. The individuals at high risk can be monitored carefully, and anyone who develops symptoms can be referred to treatment in an effort to eliminate the disorder before it becomes established.

A universal prevention program is one that is applied to an entire group of people and is designed to prevent a disease before it begins.

Universal Prevention Programs

Universal prevention programs are most successful when all the members of the group targeted are at risk for the development of the problem and the prevention program can focus on a small number of factors that clearly increase the risk. Since eating disorders are, fortunately, relatively uncommon, prevention programs targeting eating disorders are not needed by the majority of individuals—they are simply not at risk. Therefore, more recent school-based programs have aimed not only to prevent eating disorders but also to aid healthy weight management, a major challenge in our current environment.

These programs are useful but seem unlikely to dramatically affect the rates of anorexia nervosa, bulimia nervosa, and binge-eating disorder.

Targeted Prevention Programs

Most of the prevention programs that have targeted individuals who are at high risk for eating disorders and/or have already begun to exhibit symptoms have focused on older adolescents or college students. Promising results have emerged in recent years. One program, the Body Project, focuses particularly on high school and college age women with increased concerns about their shape and weight, and it aims to help them resist the social pressures to be thinner. Individuals who participate have been found to have reduced body dissatisfaction, unhealthy dieting, and symptoms of eating disorders, especially binge eating. A number of sororities in the United States have adopted the Body Project.

The Stanford Student Bodies project is an online program for students in high school or college that addresses risk factors for eating disorders and encourages the development of healthier diets and improved body image. A related program, StayingFit, has more recently been developed to teach about healthy weight regulation more generally.

These programs have been under development for a number of years and have progressively become more effective. There is good evidence that they are useful in improving attitudes about shape and weight and in reducing some symptoms of eating disorders. However, as with the universal programs, it is not clear that they significantly reduce the number of cases of anorexia nervosa, bulimia nervosa, and binge-eating disorder.

Does the Treatment of Overweight/Obesity Increase the Risk of Developing an Eating Disorder?

In *DSM-5*, obesity is not considered an eating disorder or, more broadly, a mental disorder, but rather a general medical problem. Are attempts to treat obesity, particularly attempts to diet, risk factors for the development of eating disorders? This has been a hot button topic that, for years, has caused considerable controversy among eating disorders specialists and obesity experts. The presumed association between dieting and the development of symptoms of eating disorders has led school-based eating disorder prevention programs to warn students about the ill effects of dieting. Yet obesity is a major public health problem for America's youth, and it is important to understand whether treatments for obesity, specifically recommendations that restrict caloric intake, do, in fact, increase the risk for the development of eating disorders.

> The treatment of obesity . . . is a hot button topic that, for years, has caused considerable controversy among eating disorders specialists and obesity experts.

More than 20% of American adolescents have obesity, and this number has increased substantially in recent decades. It is suspected that the majority of teenagers who are overweight will continue to have obesity as adults and will, as a result, experience increased risks of cardiovascular disease, high cholesterol, high blood pressure, diabetes mellitus, gallbladder disease, several cancers (e.g., breast and colon cancer), and psychosocial problems. Adults who were obese as teenagers suffer adverse health effects later in life, and obese teens are likely to suffer from health complications even before they reach adulthood. Type 2 ("adult-onset") diabetes, a form of diabetes that is linked to being overweight, was once rare in children and adolescents, but recent reports show that the frequency of type 2 diabetes among adolescents is increasing dramatically, with an increase of more than 30% between 2001 and 2009.

A combination of reducing calories (i.e., dieting) and increasing physical activity is the cornerstone of weight management in overweight adolescents, just as it is in adults with obesity. There is compelling evidence that even modest weight loss improves both physical and psychological health. However, as is well known, weight loss is difficult to sustain, both because the body has strong, built-in physical mechanisms that push against weight loss, such as increasing appetite, and because there are so many opportunities in the current US society to obtain inexpensive high-calorie food. Some clinicians and researchers have been concerned that encouraging dieting may increase the risk of eating disorders, particularly among adolescent females, and that weight loss programs might do more harm than good. By contrast, obesity experts generally believe that early intervention during the adolescent period is the preferred method for dealing with obesity, citing the likelihood that a teen will receive family support and encouragement to lose weight, that eating habits and other behaviors are more easily modified in a young person than they are in an adult, and that proliferation of fat tissue may be curtailed. There is no convincing evidence that appropriate, medically supervised weight loss programs lead to emotional problems or eating disorders. Early treatment of obesity may also be cost-effective. By preventing overweight children and adolescents from becoming obese adults, healthcare costs for treating obesity-related complications could be reduced.

Moreover, the vast majority of adolescent dieters don't develop eating disorders. Most teenage girls report dieting at least at some point, but only a few percent develop an eating disorder. Therefore, many more factors than simply attempting to diet contribute to the development of eating disorders. And while it's been proved that average-weight individuals do experience adverse behavioral and psychological effects from a severe restriction in calories, obese adults who have lost 10% of their initial body weight generally show improvements in mood and reductions in binge eating.

> The vast majority of adolescent dieters don't develop eating disorders.

Interventions for Overweight Children and Adolescents

Several national organizations, such as the US Preventive Services Task Force, have published recommendations regarding the treatment of youngsters who are overweight or obese. As in the treatment of anorexia nervosa and bulimia nervosa, the most effective strategies engage the parents. Effective strategies emphasize diet, physical activity, and cognitive and behavioral changes. Dietary change may include reduced calorie and fat intake, such as by avoiding highly energy-dense foods and increasing diet variety. A commonly utilized technique categorizes foods according to traffic light colors: High-calorie foods (like cookies and soda) are red and should be consumed infrequently, low-calorie foods (like most vegetables) are green and are okay to eat freely, and medium-calorie foods are yellow and can be consumed in moderation.

Programs aimed at decreasing weight sensibly rely on increasing physical activity through aerobic exercise (e.g., swimming, jogging, or basketball) as well as through lifestyle changes that increase overall activity during daily routines (e.g., using stairs rather than elevators, walking instead of driving a short distance). Such programs also encourage the reduction of sedentary behaviors, such as watching television or playing video games.

Parental involvement in the weight loss efforts of their children is essential. Parents who modify their own eating or activity habits can encourage their children to follow suit. Additionally, parents can limit high-fat and high-sugar foods available at home while encouraging their children to eat fruits, vegetables, and other healthy choices. In fact, through these and other similar methods, parents can help children not only to lose significant amounts of weight but also to maintain their reduced weight for 10 years or more.

The Effects of Dieting and Weight Loss on Eating Behavior and Psychological Status

Most studies of the impact of well-developed weight loss programs—that is, those overseen by an experienced professional such as a physician, psychologist, or nutritionist— have found that children's preoccupation with dieting, unhealthy weight loss behaviors, and concerns about being overweight either decrease or stay the same, indicating that appropriate weight loss efforts do not generally lead to an increase in eating disorder symptoms. (But, as a parent, you should keep an eye out to be sure your child is not the exception and starts to show behaviors such as extreme food avoidance or purging.)

What about the effects of dieting and weight loss on a child's emotional state? Can these precipitate such emotional reactions as depression, anxiety, and irritability, as investigators worried some years ago? In research over the past several decades, sensible dieting (such as a modest reduction in calorie intake combined with increased physical activity) has generally not been found to have a negative effect on mood. In one study, for example, participants lost an average of 20% of their weight while at the same time some aspects of their psychological status, such as social competence, improved. Another study found significant reductions in symptoms of depression and anxiety in children involved in a family-based weight control program.

> Sensible dieting has generally not been found to have a negative effect on mood.

The Bottom Line on Obesity

Our current understanding that professionally administered weight loss programs for children and adolescents who are overweight do not increase eating disorder symptoms is based on a limited number of studies. Further research is needed to reconcile the consistent finding that dieting, as practiced in behavioral weight loss programs for overweight youngsters, appears associated with improved psychological and behavioral changes with concerns that excessive dieting behavior can lead to an eating disorder. Several issues must be considered.

1. Healthy dieting, which encourages only modest caloric restriction in combination with the increased consumption of low-fat dairy products and fruits and vegetables, appears to present few risks to overweight youth. By contrast, unhealthy weight loss behaviors, which include severe caloric restriction (e.g., crash diets) and the

prohibition of certain foods (e.g., fad diets), may significantly increase the risk of eating disorders and emotional complications. This is possible in overweight youth, as well as in normal-weight adolescents, especially girls, who diet aggressively in pursuit of an ever-thinner ideal. Similarly, chronic restrained eating may pose risks that are not associated with healthy dieting.

2. Some overweight youth may be at risk for adverse behavioral consequences of dieting and weight loss even when they participate in a professionally administered program. Studies of individuals over many years, for example, have shown that severe body image dissatisfaction and weight and shape preoccupation are the most robust predictors of the development of eating disorders in adolescent girls. Thus, overweight teenagers with marked body image dissatisfaction, depression, or other emotional complications may be at greatest risk of experiencing binge eating episodes when subjected to even modest caloric restriction.

> Overweight teenagers with marked body image dissatisfaction, depression, or other psychiatric complications may be at greatest risk of experiencing binge eating episodes.

3. Weight regain is common in overweight adolescents, as it is in obese adults. In adults, weight cycling (i.e., weight loss followed by regain) does not appear to be associated with clinically significant behavioral consequences (though it certainly can be psychologically challenging), but in overweight youth with a history of psychiatric complications, weight cycling might produce different effects.

Whenever possible, follow-up assessment should be conducted through late adolescence, when symptoms of bulimia nervosa or binge-eating disorder might emerge.

Ultimately, large-scale trials are needed to determine the behavioral risks posed by different weight loss interventions for overweight youth. While health professionals, teachers, and parents will continue to be concerned about the all-too-common occurrence of misguided weight loss efforts among children and teenagers, all should be increasingly concerned about the growing epidemic of pediatric obesity. Twenty percent of America's adolescents are already overweight or obese, and, as adults, will be at increased risk of serious medical and psychosocial consequences. Concerns about the potential ill effects of dieting should not impede efforts to develop more effective methods of treating obesity among young people. Such concerns should also not discourage urgently needed efforts to prevent the development of excessive weight gain among both children and adults in the first place.

Perhaps, as in many areas of life, the best approach is one of moderation. Encouraging moderate, balanced food intake and moderate amounts of regular physical activity should be helpful in promoting a healthy lifestyle both for overweight youngsters and for those young people who tend toward the excessive caloric restriction and extreme exercise that are associated with eating disorders.

What Parents Can Do to Help Prevent Eating Disorders

The person who coined the phrase "You can never be too rich or too thin" obviously hadn't witnessed someone struggling with the devastating effects of anorexia nervosa or another eating disorder. And yet, in a world where people are now more aware of eating disorders than they were 20 years ago, there is still a reverence for thinness. According to the NEDA, Americans spend more than $40 billion dollars annually on dieting and diet-related products, which is roughly equivalent to the amount the US federal government spends on education each year.

It's no wonder the Americans shell out so much money trying to become thinner. As the average BMI and waist circumference have increased for adult American men and women, the images with which we are bombarded at every turn are increasingly unrealistic. Excruciatingly thin models, actresses, actors, and athletes grace the covers of almost every magazine produced in this country (and in other industrialized nations as well) or are featured on the inside pages, where they hawk everything from clothing to perfume to personal hygiene products. Even if you don't buy such publications, your child is still exposed to them at every street corner newsstand, in convenience stores, or next to grocery store checkout counters, not to mention online, where celebrities and cultural "influencers" populate their social media feeds with their latest diet and exercise fads. Worse yet, perhaps, are those celebrities who claim to "eat everything" and yet remain unrealistically thin.

The pervasive cultural message that to be attractive one must be thin, combined with the relentless promotion of dieting, provides a fertile environment in which eating disorders can take root in some people. What can you as a parent do to prevent the development of an eating disorder in your child? Where should you start? The NEDA recommends that the first thing you can do is to learn as much as you can about syndromes like anorexia nervosa, bulimia nervosa, and binge-eating disorder. By gaining genuine awareness, you can "avoid judgmental or mistaken attitudes about food, weight, body shape, and eating disorders."

Fortunately, since the first edition of this book, there is more content transmitting positive ideas about the reality that bodies come in all shapes and sizes. Sometimes the healthy messages are overt, as in the Netflix series *Shrill*, in which Annie (played by Aidy Bryant) is a young woman intent on changing her life—advancing in her career and making better relationship choices—while explicitly resisting messages that she needs to change her body. Sometimes the message is covert, as in the use of pictures of models who are not airbrushed, a campaign initiated by Aerie in 2016, or who represent a range of body types, a diversity embraced by companies including Aerie and Athleta. Even Barbie has a new body, and Disney has introduced with Moana a princess with a more realistic body shape! It is encouraging to see the ways that culture is catching up with the real world, but, of course, there is still a long way to go.

To understand the possible impact of the thin-ideal or diet-obsessed culture on your child, take a look at your teen's social media and entertainment diet. Who do they follow on Instagram or Facebook? Which blogs do they read? Which Netflix or Hulu series do they binge watch? Taken together, what messages are they getting from their preferred content?

It's equally important to examine your own ideas and attitudes about your body and your behavior around your children. Do you make derogatory comments about your appearance in front of your daughter? Do you make disparaging remarks about the appearance of others while out with your son? Do you point out obese people to your child and say, "If you're not careful, you're going to look like that someday?" Do you ever gossip to your children about a friend or relative looking awful because they're so fat? Such comments tell your kids that you value a person's appearance more than you do the person for who he or she is. Candy, who was obese as a teen but lost weight in her early 20s, offers an example of how much her mother's attitude affected her.

> It's . . . important to examine both your own ideas and attitudes about your body and your behavior around your children.

"My mom was very glamorous-looking in a 1940s movie-star sort of way. While I was growing up, all of my friends thought she was totally cool because she seemed so sophisticated and self-assured. What they didn't know was that every time she'd get dressed, she'd stand in front of the mirror and constantly put herself down because of her 'piano legs,' which was how she referred to her thick, stocky calves. She was so stunning that nobody else even noticed her legs, but all she could focus on was the one part of her body she felt made her imperfect. After constantly hearing her berate herself, I learned that there's always something—some part of you—that's unacceptable and makes you less of a person. Parents need to keep in mind that their kids are watching them and listening to everything they say about themselves and about others. If the comments are self-effacing or derogatory, children will assimilate those negative values."

Another key element in the prevention of eating disorders is to make sure that you as a parent don't convey the message to your child that becoming thinner is a solution to all of life's challenges. Candy again:

> "Parents need to keep in mind that their kids are watching them and listening to everything they say about themselves and about others."

"After I got really fat, my mom kept telling me that if I lost weight, I'd become the happiest girl in the whole USA. She swore that strangers on the street would stop and swoon as I walked by and boys at school would get into fights over who would take me out. In other words, in my mother's view, everything I ever dreamed of having could be attained if only I was thin. After I finally lost 100 pounds, which I did sensibly over a 3-year period, I was totally crushed because it became clear that my mother was wrong. People didn't fall down on the street as I passed by, strangers didn't knock on my door to tell me how darned good I looked, and being thinner didn't help me achieve everything I'd hoped to in life."

If your child is overweight, don't tell her there's a pot of gold at the end of the weight loss rainbow. Instead, keep the expectations reasonable. Stress improvements in physical health, mood, energy, and enjoyment of activities with friends. By presenting it in such a way, you let her know that it's more important to do something for herself rather than to please someone else or to be more attractive to another person and that there are outcomes other than weight or size that matter. The same advice also applies if your child is a boy.

Along those same lines, Shirley speaks up about a dangerous trend rapidly spreading among teenagers in this country. "Two words: cosmetic surgery," she says. "I heard on the news that a girl received breast implants for her sixteenth birthday. When her parents came under fire for giving her such a gift, their explanation was they only did it because it was what she'd asked for. Can you imagine? Her breasts aren't even fully developed yet and they buy her implants? Those parents should be ashamed of themselves, as should the doctor who performed the procedure. So, too, should parents who allow their teenagers to have nose jobs, tummy tucks, or liposuction. We all know that adolescence is an awkward time physically, but these children aren't even allowing nature to take its course. They're having their bodies altered before they've had time to grow into them, with their parents obviously approving of it by footing the bills. If this trend keeps up, everybody will have cute perky noses, cute perky breasts, and cute perky butts. How boring is that? Don't these people understand that it's natural—and wonderful—to live in a world where everybody is different?"

Does your daughter comment about how she wishes she could look like everybody else? Has she internalized "thin ideals"? If you're unsure, sit down and talk to her. Find out how she feels about what she sees every day on TV, in magazines, and on the Internet. Donna regrets not having talked more with Chelsey, who loves fashion magazines and blogs and had a picture of Kaia Gerber as the wallpaper image on her laptop.

"I didn't think much about the Kaia Gerber image at first," she says. "I know she's a popular teen model, and I figured that Chelsey really liked the outfit she was wearing because she's so into fashion design." It was only later, after her daughter was diagnosed with anorexia nervosa, that Donna discovered the real significance of the wallpaper image of Gerber. It was Chelsey's reminder of what she thought she needed to look like to be attractive and successful and served as a triggering device to keep losing weight.

"Back in my day, Kate Moss was the scary-skinny model everyone admired. The companies who used Moss in advertisements didn't think twice about what her image portrayed to young girls and women around the world. 'Be skinny and be a super-star.' Now my child was getting the same unhealthy ideas, and she was especially vulnerable to them. I made a vow to not purchase any product that's promoted with the image of an emaciated-looking person, and to support clothing lines that are making clothes for all bodies *and* showing a range of bodies on their runways. I've also told my relatives, friends, and neighbors to do the same."

Another necessary step toward the prevention of eating disorders is to educate teenagers about prejudice in its varying forms, including the bias against those who are overweight. If your son shows up one day wearing a "No Fat Chicks" t-shirt, it's definitely time for a heart-to-heart talk about the damage such an attitude can cause. The same response should be used if you hear your daughter talking to friends about how "fat and gross" a classmate is. Your children need to know that labeling people as "fat," "stupid," "geek," or "loser" serves no other purpose than to limit their opportunities to get to know people for who they really are.

Because eating disorders begin most frequently around puberty, it is essential to address the role of biology with your teen. A young girl who was formerly considered a "string bean" or a "tomboy" can suddenly become horrified by the fat that starts to grow around her hips, thighs, and buttocks. The development of breasts can also affect girls differently: some are thrilled when their chests change while others are upset about it. Boys, too, can be resistant to the changes taking place in their bodies. Whatever the case with your child, be there and be supportive, but don't impose attitudes that he or she isn't yet ready for. Even if you think it's marvelous that your child is passing from childhood to adulthood, refrain from saying things like "Look at how wonderfully you're filling out," or "I can't believe how much my little boy has grown." While seemingly innocent enough, such remarks have the potential of increasing the self-consciousness some children already feel about their changing bodies or can cause them to take drastic measures (such as self-starvation or purging) in an attempt to battle the laws of nature. Instead, talk openly and honestly with them about what to expect in the near future (e.g., that gaining weight during puberty is natural, especially for girls) and be sure to let them know that it will be many years before their bodies stop growing and changing. If you're unsure of the actual biological facts or feel you need help with how best to discuss bodily changes with your teen, ask for advice from your child's pediatrician, your own doctor, or a health education specialist.

In addition to the physical changes brought by the onset of puberty, your child faces emotional changes as well, which is why eating disorder specialists advise parents to discourage teasing someone about his or her appearance. It's true that playful teasing is part of family life; you've undoubtedly teased your children at some point, just as they've teased you. Still, if you laugh when your son calls his sister "thunder thighs" or when your daughter calls her brother "lard butt," your reaction can have a powerful negative impact on the child who's the brunt of the joke. "Fat talk," as it's been dubbed, is incredibly common within families and friend groups, with estimates suggesting that for some people as much as one-quarter of all interactions in a given week may involve some sort of appearance-related content. Fat talk, delivered in-person in the family living room or online via social media platforms, is associated with body dissatisfaction, which is in turn associated with disordered eating and exercise behavior and symptoms of depression and anxiety.

Candy relates the following story: "One day when I was about 15 and still heavy, I was walking through our living room when my brother said, 'Hey, you guys, where are you going?' I didn't really get it, but my mother started laughing hysterically. I finally figured out that he was making a joke about me being big enough to be two people. Since my brother was a stupid jerk, I could've easily blown him off if it hadn't been for the fact that my mother kept laughing. Not only that, but afterward, she told everyone she knew—relatives, friends, neighbors, even people at her job—what my brother had said. Eventually, everybody started calling me 'you guys,' too. It was totally humiliating, and I became very depressed. I mean, if your own mother doesn't mind you being ridiculed and even thinks it's funny, what can you expect from the rest of the world?"

Zach also remembers being teased, in this case for being smaller than the other boys his age. "But the worst of it was when my little sister grew taller than me and started calling me 'shrimpary' instead of Zachary because I was 'such a little shrimp.' My parents didn't do much to stop it because they understood that she was frustrated by all the ways the household revolved around my needs in terms of where and what we could eat, and now I get that, but at the time, it was embarrassing and kind of cruel."

If your children tend to tease each other unmercifully about appearance, make a point of sitting down with each of them to explain how hurtful some jokes can be and why they should remember that people are more than just their bodies. Praise your kids for who they are and what they do, not how they look.

Have you ever told your children you can't go swimming with them because you'll "look like a beached whale" in your bathing suit? Have you avoided wearing shorts and sleeveless shirts because you don't want all of your "flab" hanging out? Do you wear high-heeled shoes because they make your legs look "longer" even as they hurt your feet? Have you insisted that certain pictures not be posted on social media because you don't like how your body looks in them? If you answered "yes" to any of the previous questions, you should stop and think about how your own attitudes and behaviors affect your teenagers. If you want them to be comfortable with their appearance, it is important that you show that you are comfortable with yours as well.

If your son or daughter is involved in a sport that requires a weight limit (i.e., gymnastics, ice skating, crew, or wrestling), talk to the coach about exactly what that weight limit is and ask if there's a structured nutritional program for your child to follow. As discussed in Chapter 4, many adolescents can become obsessed with pleasing teachers and coaches and often keep dropping pounds long after they've met the sport's required weight limit. By being informed about their training regimen, you won't be susceptible to excuses like "Coach says I need to lose a few more pounds," or "The teacher told me I shouldn't eat dinner because it will make me too fat for trials." Also, if you're worried that your child might be at particular risk of developing an eating disorder, it would be wise to suggest that he or she participate in a sport that doesn't involve being a certain size or shape. When asked what she thought would help prevent eating disorders, Audra's mother Valerie said, "No school should have a weight limit for cheerleaders." While it's true that many cheerleading routines have become very complicated, with kids being thrown up into the air and squads standing on each other's shoulders, there should still be a place for everybody who wants to participate.

Michael's mother Diane suggests that one of the best ways to prevent eating disorders is to throw out your bathroom scale. "Kids with eating disorders become obsessed with the scale," she says. "Their days are dictated by how the numbers on that scale rise and fall. After Michael finally embraced recovery, the first thing I did was get rid of the scale, and I also gave away all of our full-length mirrors. If you feel good about yourself and the way you look, there's no reason to have a mirror around so that you can fret about your image."

> "The first thing I did was get rid of the scale, and I also gave away all of our full-length mirrors."

Other parents warn about the dangers of allowing your child access to everything that's posted online. Since its inception, the Internet has become a vital tool for anyone seeking information that was formerly unavailable locally. Unfortunately, the downside is the number of websites that post things vulnerable teens shouldn't see. Parents of children with eating disorders mention this issue because, several years ago, personal websites promoting anorexia nervosa and bulimia nervosa as "lifestyles" and "choices" proliferated. These sites and related social media accounts, dubbed "Pro-Ana" (pro-anorexia) and "Pro-Mia" (pro-bulimia), were created by individuals longing to make contact with others who had anorexia nervosa or bulimia nervosa. The sole purpose of this contact was to "chat" and "inspire" each other to continue the quest to be as thin as possible and/or to share tips about unhealthy behaviors like fasting or purging. Due to a huge public outcry about how harmful these sites can be, many have been shut down, yet some still remain, tweeting away, and getting daily hits from users all over the world. A recent post on one of the "Pro-Mia" sites was a question from someone who needed advice about where she could purge when the bathrooms at home were occupied. There were at least 10 responses to the question, none of which told her she shouldn't make herself throw up in the first place. Instead, the answers offered suggestions as to where she could vomit without being caught and how to get rid of the evidence later. Such posts make it obvious that people in the throes of eating disorders still do visit existing "Pro-Ana" and "Pro-Mia" sites on a regular basis. If you believe your child is susceptible to developing an eating disorder or is recovering from one, it would be wise to block access to such sites on all of the computers in your home, just as you would block hard-core porn sites, and to monitor who your teen follows on social media. If you have qualms about censorship, keep in mind that as a parent you are responsible for protecting your child from anything you deem harmful. As one mother said, "You wouldn't let your kid stand in front of an oncoming car or allow them to put their hand over an open flame, so why would you let them have access to websites that could trigger disordered eating behavior or, worse, prove fatal?"

If you want to learn more about the prevention of eating disorders, there are numerous national organizations you can contact, many of which are listed in the Resources section of this book.

Chapter Six

Conclusion

A Call for Action

S ince the first edition of this book was published in 2005, there have been significant advances not only in our understanding of the eating disorders, but also in the laws and policies governing access to their treatment. In 2008, the Mental Health Parity and Addiction Equity Act, sponsored by Senators Paul Wellstone and Pete Dominici, closed a number of loopholes in a previous parity law and thereby aimed to assure that the health insurance policies of large, employer-based group plans provided similar levels of coverage for mental healthcare as they did for medical and surgical care. In 2010, the Affordable Care Act (ACA, "Obamacare") extended mental health parity to individual policies and small group plans.

In theory, these federal laws substantially improved access to treatment for eating disorders, but, unfortunately, patients and parents have discovered that additional efforts and advocacy have been required. For example, in 2015, the office of the Attorney General of New York announced that it had received numerous complaints that a behavioral health management company (HealthNow)—a company that manages the payments for mental healthcare services covered by an insurance plan or plans—was wrongly limiting the number of treatment sessions that would be covered and excluding nutritional counseling for eating disorders. The Attorney General initiated an investigation of HealthNow, and, in 2016, the Attorney General's office announced a settlement which required HealthNow to cease its limitations on eating disorders treatment and to reimburse patients and families for costs that the company should have covered. So, there is good news and bad news: new laws now require insurers to provide better coverage for mental healthcare than in the past, including for treatment of eating disorders, but you may have to go to some lengths to be sure you receive the coverage to which you are entitled.

In many areas of the United States, it is difficult to locate treatment facilities with the resources and expertise necessary to treat eating disorders. Responding to the growing awareness of the toll often taken by these disorders, New York State has also taken a lead role in helping patients and families to identify treatment resources. In 2004, Governor George Pataki signed into law a bill that provides funding for Comprehensive Care Centers for Eating Disorders in New York State. The law, which is still in effect, authorizes funds to support three centers of excellence across the state to enhance comprehensive, coordinated, and continuous specialized treatment for eating disorders and to facilitate early intervention for those in need to avoid complications and repeated hospitalizations. Additional information is available at www.health.ny.gov.

Several national organizations have made strong efforts to aid individuals with eating disorders and their families find out about eating disorders and get access to treatment. Website and contact information for these organizations can be found in the Resources section. Briefly, NEDA is the country's largest nonprofit organization dedicated to supporting individuals and families affected by eating disorders. NEDA maintains an extensive directory of treatment resources and staffs a free helpline to assist in locating providers. Project HEAL, founded by two young women who themselves had anorexia nervosa as teenagers, aims to enhance accessibility to treatment in a number of innovative ways, including helping patients and families to get all the insurance coverage to which they are entitled and by facilitating peer support for individuals with an eating disorder from someone who has recovered.

Both NEDA and the Eating Disorder Coalition make strenuous and persistent efforts to advocate on behalf of individuals with eating disorders at the federal and state levels. These efforts include encouraging lawmakers to assure that the provisions of new legislation such as the ACA are fully extended to eating disorders and to increase funding for research on these illnesses. These, and many other organizations across the globe, join together yearly to raise awareness of eating disorders on World Eating Disorders Action Day (http://www.worldeatingdisordersday.org).

All of the programs just described were developed in response to advocacy by individuals with eating disorders and their families, proof that advocacy *works*. As individuals and as a nation we must continue this work to decrease the stigma, secrecy, and shame that accompany eating disorders so that those in need of treatment will seek it and be able to obtain it. The parents whose experiences informed the vignettes in this book have all, in their own ways, become powerful advocates for children and adolescents with eating disorders. Some have done so publicly by speaking at conferences and giving talks around the country about the dangers of eating disorders, by helping to establish charitable foundations dedicated to advancing the knowledge and treatment of these disorders, and by forming support groups in their local communities. Others have taken a more private route, working on behalf of their own children by fighting to get them the right treatment and to help them along the long road to recovery. And all, of course, have shared their experiences in this book in order to offer their practical wisdom about these illnesses to you.

> As individuals and as a nation we must continue to work to decrease the stigma, secrecy, and shame that accompany eating disorders.

Whether in small steps or large strides, all of these parents, and thousands of others whose children have been affected by these disorders, are helping to lift the silence and stigma that surround these illnesses and to change our nation's cultural and political climate so that real progress in the diagnosis, treatment, and prevention of these complex illnesses can be made. Eating disorders, as one mother put it in Chapter 4, are first and foremost "family diseases," and there are many families like your own who are dealing with them every day. In short, you and your child are not alone in your struggle to beat these illnesses. Reach out and get help. Get support from others whose lives have been touched by eating disorders, find out about the ongoing research on these disorders by consulting with experienced professionals, educate yourself about available treatments, read other books besides this one—in short, stay informed about every aspect of your child's illness and recovery, and, most important, don't give up until he or she is safely out of harm's way. You can also help your own family and others like yours by advocating for improved healthcare coverage and for more research on eating disorders. You *can* make a difference, and your child will surely benefit from your efforts in the long run.

Glossary

acute treatment Any treatment that is aimed at achieving rapid reduction of symptoms.

Affordable Care Act (ACA) A program enacted during the Obama administration that expanded medical insurance coverage and required coverage for the treatment of mental illnesses.

amenorrhea The absence of menstrual periods.

anticonvulsant A medication that helps prevent seizures. Many anticonvulsants have mood-stabilizing effects as well.

antidepressant A medication used to prevent or relieve depression.

antipsychotic A medication used to prevent or relieve psychotic symptoms. Some newer antipsychotics have mood-stabilizing effects as well.

anxiety disorder Any of several mental disorders that are characterized by extreme or maladaptive feelings of tension, fear, or worry.

atypical antipsychotic One of the newer antipsychotic medications. Some atypical antipsychotics are also used as mood stabilizers.

bipolar disorder A mood disorder characterized by an overly high mood, called mania, which alternates with depression. Also called *manic depression.*

body mass index (BMI) A measure of weight relative to height (calculated as weight in kilograms divided by height in meters squared. A calculator is available at https://www.cdc.gov/healthyweight/assessing/bmi/adult_bmi/english_bmi_calculator/bmi_calculator.html

celiac disease A digestive disorder that can result in weight loss and malnutrition.

cognitive-behavioral therapy (CBT) A form of psychotherapy that aims to correct ingrained patterns of thinking and behavior that may be contributing to a person's mental, emotional, or behavioral symptoms.

comorbidity The simultaneous presence of two or more disorders.

cortisol A hormone released by the adrenal glands that is responsible for some of the physiological effects of stress.

depression A feeling of being sad, hopeless, or apathetic that lasts for at least a couple of weeks. See also *major depression.*

diabetes A disease marked by high levels of sugar in the blood (hyperglycemia), which can be caused by too little insulin (a hormone produced by the pancreas to regulate blood sugar), resistance to insulin, or both.

***Diagnostic and Statistical Manual of Mental Disorders*, Fifth Edition (*DSM-5*)** A manual that mental health professionals use for diagnosing mental illnesses.

dialectical behavior therapy (DBT) A specific form of cognitive-behavioral therapy.

diuretic Any substance that causes increased production of urine.

eating disorder A disorder characterized by serious disturbances in eating behavior. People may severely restrict what they eat, or they may go on eating binges then attempt to compensate by such means as self-induced vomiting or misuse of laxatives.

electrolytes Salt constituents (sodium, potassium, chloride, and bicarbonate) found naturally in the bloodstream that are needed to maintain normal physical functioning.

family-based therapy Psychotherapy that brings together several members of a family for therapy sessions.

group therapy Psychotherapy that brings together several patients with similar diagnoses or issues for therapy sessions.

hospitalization Inpatient treatment in a facility that provides intensive, specialized care and close, round-the-clock monitoring.

hyperthyroidism Overactive thyroid.

hypothalamus Part of the brain that serves as the command center for the nervous and hormonal systems.

individual therapy Psychotherapy in which a patient meets one-on-one with a therapist.

inflammatory bowel disease A general term for diseases (e.g., Crohn's disease and ulcerative colitis) characterized by inflammation in the intestines/digestive tract.

interpersonal therapy (IPT) A form of psychotherapy that aims to address the interpersonal triggers for mental, emotional, or behavioral symptoms.

ipecac A substance used to induce vomiting after accidental poisoning.

laxative A substance that helps promote bowel movements.

maintenance therapy Any treatment that is aimed at preventing a recurrence of symptoms.

major depression A mood disorder that involves either being depressed or irritable nearly all the time, or losing interest or enjoyment in almost everything. These feelings last for at least 2 weeks, are associated with several other symptoms, and cause significant distress or impaired functioning.

Medicaid A government program, paid for by a combination of federal and state funds, that provides health and mental health care to low-income individuals who meet eligibility criteria.

menarche The first occurrence of menstruation during puberty.

mental health parity A policy that attempts to equalize the way that mental and physical illnesses are covered by health plans.

mental illness A mental disorder that is characterized by abnormalities in mood, emotion, thought, or higher order behaviors, such as social interaction or the planning of future activities.

monoamine oxidase inhibitor (MAOI) An older class of antidepressant, which require important dietary restrictions and have potentially severe side effects. Now rarely used.

mood A pervasive emotion that colors a person's whole view of the world.

mood disorder A mental disorder in which a disturbance in mood is the chief feature. Also called *affective disorder.*

mood stabilizer A medication for bipolar disorder that reduces manic and/or depressive symptoms and helps even out mood swings.

neurotransmitter A chemical that acts as a messenger within the brain.

obsessive-compulsive disorder (OCD) A mental disorder that is characterized by being obsessed with a certain idea and/or feeling compelled by an urgent need to engage in certain rituals.

partial hospitalization Services, such as individual and group therapy, special education, vocational training, parent counseling, and therapeutic recreational activities, that are provided for at least 4 hours per day.

pathology An abnormal condition or biological state in which proper functioning is prevented.

perfectionism A feeling that anything less than perfect is unacceptable.

personality disorders A constellation of personality traits that significantly impair one's ability to function socially or cause personal distress.

pituitary gland A small gland located at the base of the brain. Its hormones control other glands and help regulate growth, metabolism, and reproduction.

placebo A pill that looks like a real medication but does not contain an active ingredient.

postmenarcheal After the onset of menstruation.

prevalence The total number of cases of a disease existing in a given population at a given point in time or during a specified time.

Pro-Ana/Pro-Mia Terms used to describe websites that promote anorexia nervosa/bulimia nervosa as "lifestyles" and "choices" rather than as disorders or illnesses.

protective factor A characteristic that decreases a person's likelihood of developing an illness.

psychiatrist A medical doctor who specializes in the diagnosis and treatment of mental illnesses and emotional problems.

psychologist A mental health professional who provides assessment and therapy for mental and emotional disorders. Also called a *clinical psychologist.*

psychosocial Any situation in which both psychological and social factors are assumed to play a role.

psychotherapy The treatment of a mental, emotional, or behavioral disorder through "talk therapy" and other psychological techniques.

purging In the case of eating disorders, purging means to rid oneself of food eaten, either via self-induced vomiting or by using laxatives, diuretics, or enemas.

randomized controlled trial A study in which participants are randomly assigned to a treatment group or a control group. The control group typically receives either a placebo or standard care. This study design allows researchers to determine which changes in the treatment group over time are due to the treatment itself.

recurrence A repeat episode of an illness.

relapse The reemergence of symptoms after a period of remission.

remission A return to the level of functioning that existed before an illness.

residential treatment center A facility that provides round-the-clock supervision and care in a dorm-like group setting. The treatment is less medically or psychiatrically intensive than in a hospital, but the length of stay is often considerably longer.

reuptake The process by which a neurotransmitter is absorbed back into the sending branch of the nerve cell that originally released it.

risk factor A characteristic that increases a person's likelihood of developing an illness.

schizophrenia A severe form of mental illness characterized by delusions, hallucinations, or serious disturbances in speech, behavior, or emotion.

selective serotonin reuptake inhibitor (SSRI) A widely prescribed class of antidepressant.

serotonin A neurotransmitter that plays a role in mood and helps regulate sleep, appetite, and sexual drive.

side effect An unintended effect of a drug.

sociocultural Involving both social and cultural factors.

substance abuse The continued use of alcohol or other drugs despite negative consequences, such as dangerous behavior while under the influence or substance-related personal, social, or legal problems.

subtype A group that is subordinate to a larger type or class.

suicidality Suicidal thinking or behavior.

targeted prevention program A program that tries to identify those who are at high risk of developing a disorder or those who have already begun to exhibit symptoms.

temperament A person's inborn tendency to react to events in a particular way.

tricyclic antidepressant (TCA) An older class of antidepressant.

Type 1 diabetes Diabetes caused by the loss of the body's ability to make insulin. See *diabetes mellitus*.

Type 2 diabetes Diabetes caused by a relative lack of and decreased sensitivity to insulin. See *diabetes mellitus*.

universal prevention program A program intended to benefit an entire group of people, not just those identified as being at risk for developing a disorder.

Resources

Books and Other Materials

Anorexia, parents-to-parents: What we wish we had understood. Documentary. http://www.parents-to-parents.org/.

Around the dinner table. Online support forum for parents and carers of those with eating disorders, offered and moderated by Families Empowered and Supporting Treatment for Eating Disorders (FEAST). https://www.aroundthedinnertable.org/.

Berg, Frances M. *Underage and overweight: America's childhood obesity epidemic—what every parent needs to know.* New York: Hatherleigh Press, 2004.

Brown, Harriet. *Brave girl eating: A family's struggle with anorexia.* New York: HarperCollins Publishers, 2010.

Crosbie, Casie, and Wendy Sterling. *How to nourish your child through an eating disorder: A simple, plate-by-plate approach to rebuilding a healthy relationship with food.* New York: The Experiment Publishing, 2018.

Dying to be thin. NOVA/PBS documentary originally broadcast on December 12, 2000. Free online. www.pbs.org/wgbh/nova/thin/program.html.

The feed blog. A blog by the Columbia Center for Eating Disorders at the New York State Psychiatric Institute. www.thefeedblog.com.

Herrin, Marcia, and Nancy Matsumoto. *The parent's guide to childhood eating disorders: A nutritional approach to solving eating disorders.* New York: Owl Books, 2002.

Kater, Kathy. *Real kids come in all sizes: Ten essential lessons to build your child's body esteem.* New York: Broadway, 2004.

Lock, James, and Daniel Le Grange. *Help your teenager beat an eating disorder* (2nd edition). New York: Guilford Press, 2015.

Muhlheim, Lauren. *When your teen has an eating disorder: Practical strategies to help your teen recover from anorexia, bulimia, and binge eating.* Oakland, CA: New Harbinger, 2018.

Parent, educator and coach toolkits. Free educational resources by the National Eating Disorders Association. https://www.nationaleatingdisorders.org/toolkits-0.

Richardson, Brenda Lane, and Elane Rehr. *101 ways to help your daughter love her body.* New York: HarperCollins, 2001.

Staying Fit. An online Stanford School of Medicine course on how to develop and maintain healthy eating, exercise, and sleep habits. Course staff: Craig B. Taylor and Denise Wilfley. Description and enrollment information available online. https://online.stanford.edu/courses/som-y0014-staying-fit.

Teachman, Bethany A., Marlene B. Schwartz, Bonnie S. Gordic, and Brenda S. Coyle. *Helping your child overcome an eating disorder: What you can do at home.* Oakland, CA: New Harbinger Publications, 2003.

Thomas, Jennifer J., and Kamryn T. Eddy. *Cognitive-behavioral therapy for avoidant/restrictive food intake disorder: Children, adolescents, and adults.* New York: Cambridge University Press, 2019.

Thomas, Jennifer J., and Jenni Schaefer. *Almost anorexic: Is my (or my loved one's) relationship with food a problem?* Center City, MN: Hazeldon/Harvard University, 2013.

Waller, Glenn, Victoria Mountford, Rachel Lawson, Emma Gray, Helen Cordery, and Hendrik Hinrichsen. *Beating your eating disorder: A cognitive-behavioral self-help guide for adult sufferers and their carers.* Cambridge, United Kingdom: Cambridge University Press, 2010.

Resources for Information, Support, and/or Treatment Referrals

Academy for Eating Disorders (AED)
(703) 234-4079
Email: info@aedweb.org
www.aedweb.org

The Alliance for Eating Disorders Awareness
(866) 662-1235
Email: info@allianceforeatingdisorders.com
www.allianceforeatingdisorders.com/

American Academy of Child and Adolescent Psychiatry
(202) 966-7300
Email: clinical@aacap.org
www.aacap.org

American Academy of Pediatrics (AAP)
(800) 433-9016
Email: ccp@aap.org
www.aap.org

American Association of Suicidology
(202) 237-2280
www.suicidology.org

American Foundation for Suicide Prevention
(888) 333-2377
The National Suicide Prevention Lifeline: 1-800-273-TALK (8255)
Crisis Text Line: text TALK to 741741
Email: info@afsp.org
www.afsp.org

American Psychiatric Association
(703) 907-7300
Email: apa@psych.org
www.psychiatry.org

American Psychological Association
(800) 374-2721
www.apa.org

Anxiety and Depression Association of America
(240) 485-1001
Email: information@adaa.org
www.adaa.org

Association for Behavioral and Cognitive Therapies
(212) 647-1890
Email: clinical.dir@abct.org
www.abct.org

Bazelon Center for Mental Health Law
(202) 467-5730
Email: intakes@bazelon.org
www.bazelon.org

Beat Eating Disorders
0300 123-3355
Email: help@beateatingdisorders.org.uk
www.beateatingdisorders.org.uk

Centers for Medicare and Medicaid Services
Medicare Services: (800) 633-4227
Medicaid Services: Contact your State Health Department
www.cms.gov

Eating Disorders Anonymous
Email: info@eatingdisordersanonymous.org
www.eatingdisordersanonymous.org

Eating Disorders Coalition (EDC)
(202) 543-9570
www.eatingdisorderscoalition.org

Eating Disorders Referral and Information Center
www.edreferral.com

Families Empowered and Supporting Treatment for Eating Disorders (FEAST)
U.S. (855) 50-FEAST
Canada +1 647-247-1339
Australia +61 731886675
United Kingdom +44 3308280031
New Zealand +64 98875172
Israel +972 23748988
Email: info@feast-ed.org
https://www.feast-ed.org/

Food and Drug Administration
(888) 463-6332
www.fda.gov

Food and Nutrition Information Center
(301) 504-5755
Email: fnic@ars.usda.gov
www.nal.usda.gov/fnic/

International Association of Eating Disorders Professionals (IAEDP)
(800) 800-8126
www.iaedp.com

Maudsley Parents
http://www.maudsleyparents.org/

Mental Health America
(703) 684-7722
www.nmha.org

NAMI: National Alliance on Mental Illness
703-524-7600
Email: info@nami.org
www.nami.org

National Eating Disorders Association (NEDA)
(800) 931-2237
Email: info@NationalEatingDisorders.org
www.nationaleatingdisorders.org

National Eating Disorder Information Centre—Canada (NEDIC)
(866) 633-4230 (toll free in Canada) or (416) 340-4156 (Toronto)
www.nedic.ca

National Institute for Health and Care Excellence (NICE)
(0)300-323-0140
Email: nice@nice.org.uk
www.nice.org.uk

National Institute of Diabetes and Digestive and Kidney Diseases (NIDDK)
Office of Communications and Public Liaison
(800) 860-8747
Email: healthinfo@niddk.nih.gov
www.niddk.nih.gov

National Institute of Mental Health
Office of Science, Planning, and Communications
(866) 615-6464
Email: nimhinfo@nih.gov
www.nimh.nih.gov

National Institutes of Health
(301) 946-4000
www.nih.gov
(Numerous toll-free phone numbers can be found on the NIH Information Lines
    webpage at www.nih.gov/health/infoline.htm)

Obesity Society
(301) 563-6526
www.obesity.org

Office on Women's Health
(800) 994-9662
https://www.womenshealth.gov/

Project HEAL
Email: contact@theprojectheal.org
https://www.theprojectheal.org/

Society for Adolescent Health and Medicine (SAHM)
(847) 686-2246
Email: info@adolescenthealth.org
www.adolescenthealth.org

United States Department of Health and Human Services—Substance Abuse and
    Mental Health Services Administration (SAMHSA) National Mental
Health Information Center
(800) 662-4357
Email: SAMHSAInfo@samhsa.hhs.gov
www.samhsa.gov

US Academic Medical Centers for Treatment, Research, and Referrals

Center of Excellence for Eating Disorders
The University of North Carolina School of Medicine
(984) 974-3834
www.med.unc.edu/psych/eatingdisorders/

Cleveland Clinic
https://my.clevelandclinic.org/health/diseases/4152-eating-disorders
(866) 588-2264

Columbia Center for Eating Disorders
New York State Psychiatric Institute
Columbia University Irving Medical Center
(646) 774-8093
Email: edru@nyspi.columbia.edu
www.columbiapsychiatry.org/research-clinics/eating-disorders-clinic

Eating Disorder Assessment and Treatment Program
Children's Hospital of Philadelphia
(215) 590-0681
www.chop.edu/centers-programs/eating-disorder-assessment-and-treatment-
program

Eating Disorders Center for Treatment and Research
University of California San Diego
(858) 534-8019
Email: eparks@ucsd.edu
http://eatingdisorders.ucsd.edu/index.html

Eating Disorders Clinical and Research Program
Massachusetts General Hospital
(617) 726-8470
massgeneral.org/psychiatry/services/treatmentprograms.aspx?id=1136

Eating Disorders Program
Boston Children's Hospital
(617) 355-7178
Email: international.center@childrens.harvard.edu
www.childrenshospital.org/centers-and-services/programs/a-_-e/eating-
disorders-program

Eating Disorder Treatment Program
Children's Hospital Colorado
(720) 777-6200
https://www.childrenscolorado.org/doctors-and-departments/departments/psych/
programs/eating-disorders/

Eating Disorders Program
Johns Hopkins Medicine Department of Psychiatry and Behavioral Sciences
(410) 502-5467
Email: PsychiatryAdmissions@jhmi.edu
www.hopkinsmedicine.org/psychiatry/specialty_areas/eating_disorders/index.
html

Eating Disorders Program
The University of Chicago Department of Psychiatry and Behavioral
Neuroscience
(773) 702-0789
https://www.uchicagomedicine.org/conditions-services/psychiatry-and-
psychology/eating-disorders-program

Eating and Weight Disorders Program
Mount Sinai Icahn School of Medicine
(212) 659-8724
Email: EatingDisorders@mssm.edu
www.mountsinai.org/care/psychiatry/services/eating-weight-disorders/treatment

Penn State Health Children's Hospital
(717) 531-2099
https://childrens.pennstatehealth.org/eating-disorders-and-adolescent-medicine

Sanford Eating Disorders and Weight Management Center
Sanford Health
(701) 234-4111
www.sanfordhealth.org/locations/sanford-eating-disorders-and-weight-management-center

Stanford Children's Health Comprehensive Eating Disorders Program
(650) 497-2701
www.stanfordchildrens.org/en/service/eating-disorders-program

UCSF Eating Disorders Program
University of California San Francisco Department of Psychiatry
(415) 514-1074
Email: eatingdisorders@ucsf.edu
https://eatingdisorders.ucsf.edu/

Bibliography

American Psychiatric Association. (2012). Guideline Watch: Practice guideline for the treatment of patients with eating disorders (3rd edition). https://www.psychiatry.org/psychiatrists/practice/clinical-practice-guidelines.

American Psychiatric Association. (2013). *Diagnostic and statistical manual of mental disorders* (5th edition). Washington, DC: American Psychiatric Association.

Attia, E., Blackwood, K. L., Guarda, A. S., Marcus, M. D., & Rothman, R. D. (2016). Marketing residential treatment programs for eating disorders: A call for transparency. *Psychiatric Services, 67*(6), 664–666.

Attia E., Steinglass J. E., Walsh B. T., Wang Y., Wu P., Schreyer C., et al. (2019). Olanzapine versus placebo in adult outpatients with anorexia nervosa: A randomized clinical trial. *American Journal of Psychiatry, 176*(6), 449–456.

Body Project, The. http://www.bodyprojectsupport.org/resources/materials.

Bridge, J. A., Iyengar, S., Salary, C. B., Barbe, R. P., Birmaher, B., Pincus, H. A., . . . Brent, D. A. (2007). Clinical response and risk for reported suicidal ideation and suicide attempts in pediatric antidepressant treatment: A meta-analysis of randomized controlled trials. *JAMA, 297*(15), 1683–1696.

Brownell, K., & Walsh, B. T. (Eds.). (2017). *Eating disorders and obesity* (3rd edition). New York: Guilford Press.

Bryant-Waugh, R. (2019). Avoidant/restrictive food intake disorder. *Child and Adolescent Psychiatric Clinics of North America, 28*(4), 557–565.

Bulik, C. M., Blake, L., & Austin, J. (2019). Genetics of eating disorders: What the clinician needs to know. *Psychiatry Clinics of North America, 42*(1), 59–73.

Byrne, S., & McLean, N. (2001). Eating disorders in athletes: A review of the literature. *Journal of Science and Medicine in Sport, 4*(2), 145–159.

Deierlein, A. L., Malkan, A., Litvak, J., & Parekh, N. (2019). Weight perception, weight control intentions, and dietary intakes among adolescents ages

10–15 years in the United States. *International Journal of Environmental Research and Public Health, 16*(6), 990.

Department of Health and Human Services, Health Care Financing Administration. Protecting your health insurance coverage. (2000). https://www.cms.gov/Regulations-and-Guidance/Health-Insurance-Reform/HealthInsReformforConsume/Downloads/protect.pdf.

Dietary Guidelines Advisory Committee. (2015). Scientific Report of the 2015 Dietary Guidelines Advisory Committee: Advisory report to the Secretary of Health and Human Services and the Secretary of Agriculture. Washington, DC: US Department of Agriculture, Agricultural Research Service.

Eisenberg, M. E., & Neumark-Sztainer, D. (2010). Friends' dieting and disordered eating behaviors among adolescents five years later: Findings from Project EAT. *Journal of Adolescent Health, 47*, 67–73.

Epstein, L. H., Valoski, A., Wing, R. R., & McCurley, J. (1990). Ten-year follow-up of behavioral, family-based treatment for obese children. *JAMA, 264*(19), 2519–2523.

Evans, D. L., Foa, E. B., Gur, R. E., Hendin, H., O'Brien, C. P., Seligman, M. E. P., & Walsh, B. T. (Eds.). (2017). *Treating and preventing adolescent mental health disorders: What we know and what we don't know—a research agenda for improving the mental health of our youth* (2nd edition). New York: Oxford University Press with the Annenberg Foundation Trust at Sunnylands and the Annenberg Public Policy Center at the University of Pennsylvania.

Foerde, K., Steinglass, J. E., Shohamy, D., & Walsh, B. T. (2015). Neural mechanisms supporting maladaptive food choices in anorexia nervosa. *Nature Neuroscience, 18*, 1571–1573.

Goldschmidt, A. B., Wall, M. M., Loth, K. A., & Neumark-Sztainer, D. (2015). Risk factors for disordered eating in overweight adolescents and young adults. *Journal of Pediatric Psychology, 40*, 1048–1055.

Gorrell, S., & Le Grange, D. (2019). Updates on treatments for adolescent bulimia nervosa. *Child and Adolescent Psychiatric Clinics of North America, 28*(4), 537–547.

Guarda, A. S., Wonderlich, S., Kaye, W., & Attia, E. (2018). A path to defining excellence in intensive treatment for eating disorders. *International Journal of Eating Disorders, 51*(9), 1051–1055.

Haines, J., Kleinman, K. P., Rifas-Shiman, S. L., Field, A. E., & Austin, S. B. (2010). Examination of shared risk and protective factors for overweight and disordered eating among adolescents. *Archives of Pediatric and Adolescent Medicine, 164*(4), 336–343.

Hales, C. M., Carroll, M. D., Fryar, C. D., & Ogden, C. L. (2017). *Prevalence of obesity among adults and youth: United States, 2015–2016.* National Center for Health Statistics Data Brief, No. 288. Hyattsville, MD: National Center for Health Statistics.

Hudson, J. I., Hiripi, E., Pope, H. G., Jr, & Kessler, R. C. (2007). The prevalence and correlates of eating disorders in the National Comorbidity Survey Replication. *Biological Psychiatry, 61*(3), 348–358.

Hudson, J. I., McElroy, S. L., Ferreira-Cornwell, M. C., Radewonuk, J., & Gasior M. (2017). Efficacy of lisdexamfetamine in adults with moderate to severe binge-eating disorder: A randomized clinical trial. *JAMA Psychiatry, 74*(9), 903–910.

Hudson, J. I., & Pope, H. G. (2017). Psychopharmacological treatment of binge eating disorder. In K. D. Brownell & B. T. Walsh (Eds.), *Eating disorders and obesity* (3rd edition) (pp. 308–313). New York: Guilford.

Hughes, E. K., Burton, C., Le Grange, D., & Sawyer, S. M. (2018). The participation of mothers, fathers, and siblings in family-based treatment for adolescent anorexia nervosa. *Journal of Clinical Child and Adolescent Psychology, 47*(sup1), S456–466.

Jebeile, H., Gow, M. L., Baur, L. A., Garnett, S. P., Paxton, S. J., & Lister, N. B. (2019, September 16). Association of pediatric obesity treatment, including a dietary component, with change in depression and anxiety: A systematic review and meta-analysis. *JAMA Pediatrics*, e192841. doi: 10.1001/jamapediatrics.2019.2841.

Jones, B. A., Haycraft, E., Murjan, S., & Arcelus, J. (2016). Body dissatisfaction and disordered eating in trans people: A systematic review of the literature. *International Review of Psychiatry, 28*(1), 81–94.

Kaplan, A. S., Walsh, B. T., Olmsted, M., Attia, E., Carter, J. C., Devlin, M. J., . . . Parides, M. (2009). The slippery slope: Prediction of successful weight maintenance in anorexia nervosa. *Psychological Medicine, 39*(6), 1037–1045.

Kaye, W. H., Wierenga, C. E., Bailer, U. F., Simmons, A. N., & Bischoff-Grethe, A. (2013). Nothing tastes as good as skinny feels: The neurobiology of anorexia nervosa. *Trends in Neuroscience, 36*(2), 110–120.

Keel, P. K. (2019). Purging disorder: Recent advances and future challenges. *Current Opinion in Psychiatry, 32*(6), 518–524.

Keel, P. K., & Forney, K. J. (2013). Psychosocial risk factors for eating disorders. *International Journal of Eating Disorders, 46*(5), 433–439.

Keel, P. K., Forney, K. J., Brown, T. A., & Heatherton, T. F. (2013). Influence of college peers on disordered eating in women and men at 10-year follow-up. *Journal of abnormal psychology, 122*(1), 105–110.

Keel, P. K., Mitchell, J. E., Miller, K. B., Davis, T. L., & Crow, S. J. (1999). Long-term outcome of bulimia nervosa. *Archives of General Psychiatry, 56*(1), 63–69.

Kotler, L., Devlin, M. J., Davies, M., & Walsh, B. T. (2003). An open trial of fluoxetine for adolescents with bulimia nervosa. *Journal of Child and Adolescent Psychopharmacology, 13*(3), 329–335.

Lascar, N., Brown, J., Pattison, H., Barnett, A. H., Bailey, C. J., & Bellary, S. (2018). Type 2 diabetes in adolescents and young adults. *Lancet Diabetes and Endocrinology, 6*(1), 69–80.

Lawman, H. G., & Ogden, C. L. (2017). Prevalence and demographics of obesity in the United States. In K. D. Brownell & B. T. Walsh (Eds.), *Eating disorders and obesity* (3rd edition) (pp. 368–373). New York: Guilford.

Le Grange, D., Hughes, E. K., Court, A., Yeo, M., Crosby, R. D., & Sawyer, S. M. (2016). Randomized clinical trial of parent-focused treatment and family-based treatment for adolescent anorexia nervosa. *Journal of American Academy of Child and Adolescent Psychiatry, 55*(8), 683–692.

Leon, A. C. (2007). The revised warning for antidepressants and suicidality: Unveiling the black box of statistical analyses. *American Journal of Psychiatry, 164*, 1786–1789.

Lock, J. (2018). Family therapy for eating disorders in youth: Current confusions, advances, and new directions. *Current Opinion in Psychiatry, 31*(6), 431–435.

Lock, J., & Le Grange, D. (2012). *Treatment manual for anorexia nervosa: A family-based approach* (2nd edition). New York: Guilford Press.

Lock, J., & Le Grange, D. (2015). *Help your teenager beat an eating disorder* (2nd edition). New York: Guilford Press.

Lydecker, J. A., Riley, K. E., & Grilo, C. M. (2018). Associations of parents' self, child, and other "fat talk" with child eating behaviors and weight. *International Journal of Eating Disorders, 51*(6), 527–534.

Mayer, L. E. S. (2017). Psychopharmacological treatment of anorexia nervosa and bulimia nervosa. In K. D. Brownell & B. T. Walsh (Eds.), *Eating disorders and obesity* (3rd edition) (pp. 302–307). New York: Guilford.

Mingoia, J., Hutchinson, A. D., Wilson, C., & Gleaves, D. H. (2017). The Relationship between social networking site use and the internalization of a thin ideal in females: A meta-analytic review. *Frontiers in Psychology, 8*, 1351.

Muhlheim, L. (2018). *When your teen has an eating disorder: Practical strategies to help your teen recover from anorexia, bulimia, and binge eating*. Oakland, CA: New Harbinger.

National Institute for Clinical Excellence. (2017). Eating disorders: Recognition and treatment. https://www.nice.org.uk/guidance/ng69.

National Task Force on the Prevention and Treatment of Obesity. (2000). Dieting and the development of eating disorders in overweight and obese adults. *Archives of Internal Medicine, 160*(17), 2581–2589.

NCHS. National Center for Health Statistics. Health, United States, 2016: With Chartbook on Long-term Trends in Health. Hyattsville, MD. 2017.

Neumark-Sztainer, D., Story, M., Dixon, L. B., & Murray, D. M. (1998). Adolescents engaging in unhealthy weight control behaviors: Are they at risk for other health-compromising behaviors? *American Journal of Public Health, 88*(6), 952–955.

Neumark-Sztainer, D., Story, M., Hannan, P. J., Perry, C. L., & Irving, L. M. (2002). Weight-related concerns and behaviors among overweight and non-overweight adolescents: Implications for preventing weight-related disorders. *Archives of Pediatric and Adolescent Medicine, 156*(2), 71–78.

Neumark-Sztainer, D., Wall, M., Larson, N. I., Eisenberg, M. E., & Loth, K. (2011). Dieting and disordered eating behaviors from adolescence to young adulthood: Findings from a 10-year longitudinal study. *Journal of the American Dietetic Association, 111*(7), 1004–1011.

Ousley, L., Cordero, E. D., & White, S. (2008). Fat talk among college students: How undergraduates communicate regarding food and body weight, shape & appearance. *Eating Disorders, 16*(1), 73–84.

Ousley, L., Cordero, E. D., & White, S. (2008). Fat talk among college students: How undergraduates communicate regarding food and body weight, shape and appearance. *Eating Disorders, 16*(1), 73–84.

Recovery Record. Mobile application software.

Rise Up + Recover. Recovery Warriors, LLC. Mobile application software.

Sawyer, S. M., Whitelaw, M., Le Grange, D., Yeo, M., & Hughes, E. K. (2016). Physical and psychological morbidity in adolescents with atypical anorexia nervosa. *Pediatrics, 137*(4), e20154080.

Sidani, J. E., Shensa, A., Hoffman, B., Hanmer, J., & Primack, B. A. (2016). The association between social media use and eating concerns among US young adults. *Journal of the Academy of Nutrition and Dietetics, 116*(9), 1465–1472.

Skemp-Arlt, K. M., Rees, K. S., Mikat, R. P., & Seebach, E. E. (2006). Body image dissatisfaction among third, fourth, and fifth grade children. *Californian Journal of Health Promotion, 4*(3), 58–67.

Smith, A. R., Zuromski, K. L., & Dodd, D. R. (2018). Eating disorders and suicidality: What we know, what we don't know, and suggestions for future research. *Current Opinion in Psychology, 22*, 63–67.

Society for Adolescent Health and Medicine, . . . Golden, N. H., Katzman, D. K., Sawyer, S. M., Ornstein, R. M., Rome, E. S., Garber, A. K., Kohn, M., & Kreipe, R. E. (2015). Position paper of the Society for Adolescent Health and Medicine: Medical management of restrictive eating disorders in adolescents and young adults. *Journal of Adolescent Health, 56*(1), 121–125.

Sonneville, K. R., Horton, N. J., Micali, N., Crosby, R. D., Swanson, S. S., Solmi, F., & Field, A. E. (2013). Longitudinal associations between binge eating and overeating and adverse outcomes among adolescents and young adults: Does loss of control matter? *JAMA Pediatrics, 167*(2), 149–155.

StayingFit. https://online.stanford.edu/courses/som-y0014-staying-fit.

Steinglass, J. E., Berner, L. A., & Attia, E. (2019). Cognitive neuroscience of eating disorders. *Psychiatric Clinics of North America, 42*(1), 75–91.

Steinhausen, H. C. (2009). Outcome of eating disorders. *Child and Adolescent Psychiatric Clinics of North America, 18*(1), 225–242.

Stice, E. (2002). Risk and maintenance factors for eating pathology: A meta-analytic review. *Psychological Bulletin, 128*, 825–848.

Sullivan, P. F. (1995). Mortality in anorexia nervosa. *American Journal of Psychiatry, 152*(7), 1073–1074.

Swanson, S. A., Crow, S. J., Le Grange, D., Swendsen, J., & Merikangas, K. R. (2011). Prevalence and correlates of eating disorders in adolescents: Results from the National Comorbidity Survey Replication Adolescent Supplement. *Archives of General Psychiatry, 68*(7), 714–723.

Tanofsky-Kraff, M., Shomaker, L. B., Wilfley, D. E., Young, J. F., Sbrocco, T., Stephens, M., Ranzenhofer, L. M., . . . Yanovski, J. A. (2014). Targeted prevention of excess weight gain and eating disorders in high-risk adolescent girls: A randomized controlled trial. *American Journal of Clinical Nutrition, 100*(4), 1010–1018.

Taylor, C. B., Bryson, S., Luce, K. H., Cunning, D., Doyle, A. C., Abascal, L. B., & Wilfley, D. E. (2006). Prevention of eating disorders in at-risk college-age women. *Archives of General Psychiatry, 63*(8), 881–888.

Thomas, J. J., & Schaefer, J. (2013). *Almost anorexic: Is my (or my loved one's) relationship with food a problem?* Center City, MN: Hazeldon/Harvard University Press.

Thomas, J. J., Wons, O. B., & Eddy, K. T. (2018). Cognitive-behavioral treatment of avoidant/restrictive food intake disorder. *Current Opinions in Psychiatry, 31*(6), 425–430.

Tosi, M., Maslyanskaya, S., Dodson, N. A., & Coupey, S. M. (2019). The female athlete triad: A comparison of knowledge and risk in adolescent and young adult figure skaters, dancers, and runners. *Journal of Pediatric and Adolescent Gynecology, 32*(2), 165–169.

Trottier, K., & MacDonald, D. E. (2017). Update on psychological trauma, other severe adverse experiences and eating disorders: State of the research and future research directions. *Current Psychiatry Reports, 19*(8), 45.

Udo, T., & Grilo, C. M. (2018). Prevalence and correlates of DSM-5-defined eating disorders in a nationally representative sample of US adults. *Biological Psychiatry, 84*(5), 345–354.

US Preventive Services Task Force. (2017). Screening for obesity in children and adolescents: Recommendation statement. *JAMA, 317*(23), 2417–2426.

Wagner, A. F., & Vitousek, K. M. (2019). Personality variables and eating pathology. *Psychiatric Clinics of North America, 42*(1), 105–119.

Waller, G., Mountford, V., Lawson, R., Gray, E., Cordery, H., & Hinrichsen, H. (2010). *Beating your eating disorder: A cognitive-behavioral self-help guide for adult sufferers and their carers.* Cambridge: Cambridge University Press.

Walsh, B.T., Attia, E., & Glasofer, D.R. (2020). *Eating disorders: What everyone needs to know.* New York: Oxford University Press.

Walsh, B. T., Attia, E., Glasofer, D. R., & Sysko R. (Eds.). (2016). *Handbook of assessment and treatment of eating disorders.* Washington, DC: American Psychiatric Association.

Whiteford H. A., Degenhardt L., Rehm J., Baxter A. J., Ferrari A. J., Erskine H. E., & Johns N. (2013). Global burden of disease attributable to mental and substance use disorders: Findings from the Global Burden of Disease Study 2010. *Lancet, 382*(9904), 1575–1586.

Wilfley, D. E., & Eichen, D. M. (2017). Interpersonal psychotherapy. In K. D. Brownell & B. T. Walsh (Eds.), *Eating disorders and obesity* (pp. 290–295). New York: Guilford.

Zimmerman, J., & Fisher, M. (2017). Avoidant/restrictive food intake disorder. *Current Problems in Pediatric and Adolescent Health Care, 47*(4), 95–103.

Index

Tables and figures are indicated by *t* and *f* following the page number

For the benefit of digital users, indexed terms that span two pages (e.g., 52–53) may, on occasion, appear on only one of those pages.